Growing as a Stepmom—with God's Help!

Growing as a Stepmom—with God's Help!

Jacqueline Syrup Bergan

theWORD
among us®

The Word Among Us
9639 Doctor Perry Road
Ijamsville, Maryland 21754
www.wordamongus.org
ISBN: 1-59325-053-3

Cover and book design by David Crosson
Cover art by Jim Higgins

Scripture passages contained herein are from the New Revised Standard
Version Bible: Catholic Edition, copyright 1989, 1993, by the Division of
Christian Education of the National Council of the Churches of Christ in the
United States of America. Used by permission. All rights reserved.

Made and printed in the United States of America

Library of Congress Cataloging-in-Publication Data
Bergan, Jacqueline Syrup.
Growing as a stepmom—with God's help! / Jacqueline Syrup Bergan.
p. cm.
Includes bibliographical references.
ISBN 1-59325-053-3 (alk. paper)
1. Stepmothers—Religious life. 2. Christian women—Religious life. I.
Title.
BV4529.18.B47 2005
248.8'431—dc

2005003953

Contents

About the Cover

The image of the mother duck with her errant ducklings always makes me smile. Somehow it resonates with my experience of being a stepmother. However, this mother duck can inspire us.

Since ancient times, in art, myth, and literature, birds have been associated with the divine and have been viewed as symbols of goodness and joy. Throughout the centuries, Christians have been spiritually uplifted by the symbol of the Holy Spirit as a dove. Another beautiful example is the resurrection symbolism of the phoenix bird rising from the ashes of death to new life.

Water birds have a special significance. In ancient art they were associated with the feminine and with nurturing. Moving as they do across water, land, and air, they are symbols of transcendence and self-realization. The duck has it all! She can swim in the water, walk on the land, and fly in the air!

As stepmothers, we can look to the lovely mother duck. We can transcend the fears and apprehensions that we may harbor about undertaking this privileged calling. We can realize our hopes and dreams of becoming loving, nurturing stepmoms. As we cling to our loving God, we are capable of traversing this journey!

Dedicated to my beloved husband, Leonard,
and to our sons and daughters:
Barry, Bridgett, Cynthia, Bart, Stacy, John, Thomas, and James

With love, Jacqueline

Introduction

Christmas Eve, 1972. Wrapped in my husband's old mackinaw, I sat on a pile of straw in a small lean-to in our backyard. The crisp, bitterly cold Minnesota night air bit into my face and into my fingers, which were wrapped around a cooling cup of hot chocolate. I felt so alone. As if in sympathy, my dog whimpered and put a paw on my shoe.

"God," I whispered into the dark night, "God, where are you? I don't know if I can do this. How did I get here? Are you there? I feel so alone."

I know now that I was not alone. There are many women, like myself, who have fallen in love and married a man who has children from a previous marriage. As stepmothers, we face the daunting task of nurturing another woman's children. Although it is apparent that the number of stepmothers is increasing, it is unfortunate that statistical information on the number of stepmothers or stepchildren in our country is unavailable. The U.S. Census Bureau doesn't provide this information. The best figures available are 1988 to 1990 estimates of the number marriages, divorces, and remarriages. On the basis of those statistics, researchers estimate that nearly one-third of all children and two-thirds of all women are likely to spend some time in a stepfamily.[1] It is clear that I am not alone!

But that night I felt very alone. In the weeks and months and years ahead, I would reach out to friends, to books, to counselors, to God in prayer.

This book is about the road I traveled from that Christmas to now.

As I considered how best to proceed in writing this book, I thought of what I would want to say to my own daughter if she were on the threshold of becoming a stepmother. I have written honestly and from my heart about the personal growth that is needed to move from recognizing and reconciling our limitations to discovering and affirming our strengths.

However, the primary focus and common thread throughout the book is that God is always present in loving and creative ways in the midst of our ordinary circumstances—in the complexities, joys, and pain of living in a stepfamily. My sincere desire is to offer hope, support, and encouragement to stepmoms, to help you grow in the knowledge of how God is working in your lives, and to help you grasp more profoundly how God's life merges with your own.

I have addressed what I consider to be the most difficult issues women face as stepmothers. In offering suggestions of how to approach stepmothering, I offer the results and recommendations of recent studies as well as what I have learned from my thirty-two years' experience as a stepmother—from my failures as well as my successes. And, since prayer has played the most important role in guiding me on my journey as a stepmother, I suggest a variety of ways to pray that have the potential of deepening your awareness of God's active presence within the events and circumstances of your own life. I want each stepmother to know that your life, lived obediently and sincerely in the light of God's will for you, will bear fruit for your husband, your children, and yourself. I believe that marriage and stepmothering will be the transformative journey by which you will grow into all that God intends and wishes you to be.

Our culture has never been in such dire need of strong and loving families. For better or for worse, we as stepmothers shape the environment around us. That environment becomes a part of us, our families, and ultimately our world. Stepmothers are in a unique position to create an environment of love that will nurture children whose lives have been broken by death or divorce. The environment we create has the potential of restoring wholeness to the children in binuclear families. Stepmothering is a holy endeavor. The hope that I might in some way help and support you in your role as a stepmother has inspired and sustained me throughout the writing of this book.

Jacqueline Syrup Bergan
Spring 2005

NOTES

1. Stepfamily Association of America, "Stepfamily Facts," www.saafamilies.org/faqs/.

CHAPTER 1

Saying Yes to Love

In the beginning was the Word. . . . (John 1:1)
. . . and the Word was love.

It is in the word of love that our journey, as stepmothers, begins. Love is the most powerful force in the universe. It comes from God and is the manifestation of God in our world. Love is the personal, central, and ultimate reality that continually calls us to God and to union and fulfillment. It is powerfully expressed in the love between a man and a woman.

Romantic love is always a surprise. It may descend slowly like a gentle spring rain, or it may strike suddenly like lightning. It is a miraculous phenomenon that simultaneously gives its recipients exuberant well-being and profound humility: "He loves me! How could he possibly love me?"

There is nothing quite as sweet as the first flush of love, unless of course one considers the dearness of lifelong fidelity. There is a preciousness in the dawning of new love, an absolute preciousness that defies the fading of time. The energy of that moment in our history continually and forever gives us life.

Remember the first time you realized that you loved your husband, the first time your heart spoke those words, "I love you"? Savor the memory. Where were you? What quality in him first attracted you? Were you resistant, or were you immediately open to love, open to giving and receiving love?

After my divorce, I was very resistant to a new love relationship. I think most women who have been divorced or who have experienced the death of a spouse are guarded. The loss of naiveté and heightened vulnerability make us wary!

I had made a colossal effort to put my life together after my divorce and wasn't looking for anyone to "mess it up"! I was happy and looked forward to a peaceful new beginning. After finishing two years of grueling graduate education to acquire certification as a registered nurse anesthetist, I settled with my three sons in a small Minnesota community. I purchased a small but lovely old house on a large corner lot with a gorgeous weeping birch in front. I loved our new home. It was cottage quaint, complete with mullioned windows and screened porch. In many ways, it was my first real home.

Then it happened. Ironically, it was on the first day of my new job that I met Leonard. Here I was, just getting my new life started, and there *he* was! When I arrived home that afternoon, flowers had been delivered and the phone was ringing. He invited me to dinner. I politely thanked him, but told him "no thanks." I was busy. That was the first of many phone calls, many dinner invitations, and many refusals. I was, however, willing to talk to him, and we visited on the phone almost every evening. We had long conversations in which we shared our lives with each other. He told me that his wife had been ill with lung cancer and had died seven months before, leaving him with five children: Barry, eighteen; Bridgett, sixteen; Cynthia, fifteen; Bart, thirteen, and Stacy, eleven. I, in turn, told him about myself and my sons: John, eleven; Thomas, seven; and James, four. I shared the difficult struggle of my divorce and my dreams of making a new life for my sons and myself. Leonard and I discovered similarities in our backgrounds: We were both Catholic, grew up on farms in North Dakota, and had a common love of the land. I enjoyed our conversations and looked forward to them. I thought he was pleasant, but I had absolutely no interest in a romantic relationship with him.

Our telephone visits continued. After a couple of months of countless refusals on my part, Leonard became angry. "For Pete's sake, I am not asking you to marry me. I am just asking you to have dinner with me!" I coyly replied, "I'll have dinner with you, you will really like me, and then where will we be?" He laughed and firmly declared that since he knew I was the answer to his prayers, he would wait for me. I did my best to convince him that I was not interested, that he should direct his prayers in another direction.

Eventually I did go out to dinner with Leonard. I still remember that first dinner. Across the table I looked at him; he possessed a quality of distinction. He was handsome. I loved the way he carried himself with a mature and poised confidence. "This isn't all bad," I told myself. Actually, we were thrilled with each other. After that first evening, our relationship developed quickly; it was like a lightning bolt. All resistance melted away. Seven months later, Leonard and I were married.

Just married, with eight children! Any marriage brings change and requires adjustments, but a marriage with a combined family—especially one as large as ours—is the bearer of enormous change and requires extraordinary adjustments. My honeymoon peignoir was quickly replaced by the garment of self-doubt!

It was easy to say yes to Leonard; the next step of accepting and saying yes to his children and everything that entailed was anything but easy. I am sure every stepmother asks, "How can this be? How can I do this? These are not my children. I did not give birth to them. I don't know how to nurture them."

In those first days, months, even years, I asked myself those questions over and over. It seemed impossible at times, but it was not impossible. I felt alone, but I was not alone. Gradually, I came to see that God, who had given us this magnificent gift of love, was going to continue to be present and active within it. The call was, and still is, to believe and trust in God's presence.

We are not the first women to say, "How can this be? How can I do such an impossible thing?" Two thousand years ago an extraordinary event occurred: the birth of God's love into the world. A young woman was called to bring forth this love. She fearfully responded, "How can this be?" She was reassured by the words of the angel, "Do not be afraid, Mary. . . . The Holy Spirit will come upon you, and the power of the Most High will overshadow you" (Luke 1:34-35).

As women of our time, we too are being called to give birth to love. Our world is desperately in need of the feminine; the gift each of us has to offer is essential. Some will express their lives and give birth to love through marriage and/or motherhood, some by a life lived in celibate sisterhood or a single life of dedicated professional service. An increasing number of women in our contemporary culture undertake the difficult task of stepmothering. It is never easy to give oneself away in love, to respond fully. Every expression and commitment of love has complexities and makes unreasonable demands. Every act of love involves labor and birth. In terms of emotional expenditure, stepmothering is labor intensive!

In his wedding homilies, French priest and theologian Pierre Teilhard de Chardin counseled newly married couples to believe in the support of God and the Holy Spirit. He emphasized that when a couple believed deeply in the Spirit's presence in their marriage, the Spirit would inspire and empower them to come to know each other through a constant exchange of their thoughts, affection, dreams, and prayers. In doing so, their marriage would be not a closed embrace but instead would reflect an expansive joy and freedom.[1]

Such advice is important for all couples, but for those of us who enter into a marriage where there are already children—for those of us who are stepmothers—it is particularly significant. The strength and power we need as stepmothers comes when our hearts are firmly grounded in the Spirit and in love.

Listen carefully. Within each of our hearts there is an angel whispering words of reassurance:

The Holy Spirit will come upon you and the power of the Most High will overshadow you; . . . for nothing will be impossible with God. (Luke 1:35, 37)

We, like Mary, can courageously say yes to love.

For Your Personal Growth

Exercise:
Imagine yourself on your wedding day. See yourself standing with your new husband before the altar. Hear yourself say, "I do." Throughout the day gently repeat the words "I do" over and over again.

Scripture:
Prayerfully read and reread Luke 1:26-38:

In the sixth month the angel Gabriel was sent by God to a town in Galilee called Nazareth, to a virgin engaged to a man whose name was Joseph, of the house of David. The virgin's name was Mary. And he came to her and said, "Greetings, favored one! The Lord is with you." But she was much perplexed by his words and pondered what sort of greeting this might be. The angel said to her, "Do not be afraid, Mary, for you have found favor with God. And now, you will conceive in your womb and bear a son, and you will name him Jesus. He will be great, and will be called the Son of the Most High, and the Lord God will give to him the throne of his ancestor David. He will reign over the house of Jacob forever, and of his kingdom there will be no end." Mary said to the angel, "How can this be, since I am a virgin?" The angel said to her, "The Holy Spirit will come upon you, and the power of the Most High will overshadow you; therefore the child to be born will be holy; he will be called Son of God. And now, your relative Elizabeth in her old age has also conceived a son; and this is the sixth month for her who was said to be barren. For nothing will be impossible with God." Then Mary said, "Here am I, the servant of the Lord; let it be with me according to your word."

NOTES

1. André Dupleix, *15 Days of Prayer with Pierre Teilhard de Chardin* (Liguori, Mo.: Liguori Publications, 1999), 30–31.

Chapter 2

Welcome Home

We all long for a home, a nurturing cocoon in which we feel safe, a place where we can be most truly who we are, where we can grow into the wholeness of being that God intends for us. In the deepest center of who we are, a small ardent voice speaks our longing for "home." It is this longing that gave so much power to the movie *E.T.*

In her thought-provoking book, *House as a Mirror of Self*, Clare Cooper Marcus writes of the profound significance of our home environment. Where we live and what we surround ourselves with greatly influence how we grow as a person. Our home and the objects within it exert a powerful effect on our path to wholeness and serve as a reflection of the process.[1] As she observes, "It may be that what a home symbolizes for each person is more critical than almost any issue."[2]

His, Mine, or Ours

The intimacy of sharing a home is a momentous undertaking for a binuclear family. Their very first decision may well be the most difficult one they ever have to make: Where will the new family live? Do you move into his house? Does he move into your house? Do all of you move into a new house? This is an extremely sensitive issue that must be negotiated with great care. The irony is that in most cases there is no choice. The size of the house will most likely determine where the family will live. Moving to a new house, which would be new territory for everyone and where no one would be intruding or invaded, would seem to be the best scenario. I suspect, however, that most remarried couples don't have the resources to purchase a significantly larger home. Combining two nuclear families is, in itself, a large financial commitment; most couples would be cautious regarding further extension of financial responsibility. The lesser of two evils is often what is left. One family has to move in, and one family has to move over. It is not an easy process!

My heart aches when I remember the time one of my stepchildren said to me, "I not only lost my mother, I also lost my home." My heart also aches for my three sons whom I moved from their home, where they felt safe, into the home of near strangers. It was very traumatic for both families. I feel anguished at the memory of it.

In the long run I think that my husband and I made the right decision about where to live. Buying or building a new house would not have been in the best interest of our family. Not only would it have been imprudent financially, but more important, it would have taken our focus away from the needs of the children. Together we now had eight children, all of whom were grieving. Our children needed our love and attention! It would have been a major distraction to build or buy a new home.

Even though I feel, in light of our situation, that we made the right decision, I nevertheless wish we would have been more sensitive. I think that the children would have benefited if we had given them a greater opportunity to express their feelings and, as far as it was appropriate, to participate in the decisions surrounding the move. Over time our children did make an excellent adjustment, but I deeply regret the suffering they endured in the process.

Each couple must negotiate its own way through this complex issue of where to live. Although each family has its own set of circumstances that need to be addressed, caution, kindness, and care for all the members of the family should guide their decision.

Making a House a Home

Sharing a home as a binuclear family requires blending the preferences of the subfamilies. The families can be very different aesthetically, and they may have extreme differences in lifestyle. One subfamily might take great pride in their yard and garden, while the other is accustomed to playing badminton on a beaten down front lawn. One may have grown up with the sound of Chopin, while the other's ears were trained to the warble of Randy Travis. Living in an unfamiliar environment with near strangers feels like being exiled in a strange land, foreign and homeless.

The home of our childhood is the place where we first get in touch with our deepest selves; what our home is like helps to form us into the people we will become. As mothers and stepmothers we have a responsibility to consider thoughtfully what we can do to make sharing a home harmonious and nurturing for our children and stepchildren. In the end, the appearance or location of the house is much less important than the amount of love and warmth within it. It is important that we create a home for the children that is warm and cozy, a home that has symbols and pictures that speak to them of family, history, and permanence. There is much we can do to help our children and stepchildren adjust to sharing a home. If our hearts are open and sensitive, our intuition will reveal the wisdom of what we can do.

Our Memories of "Home." Each of us has memories of our favorite childhood home or special place that we cherish. By recalling what we most loved about the special place that we called home, we will receive clues about how we can create a home that our combined family will cherish as well.

I lived a significant portion of my childhood on my grandmother's farm. It is my memory of those happy times that most evokes the feeling of home for me. I loved the summer days spent working with my grandmother in the flower garden. I loved the cold days spent sitting with her beside the warmth of the wood-burning stove. I looked forward to the early mornings when she taught me the art and joy of making and kneading bread. The aroma of bread baking in the afternoon seemed to permeate and warm the entire house; the remembrance of it continues to comfort me. Then of course there was the moment of reward when the steaming bread came out of the oven, warm and golden brown. My grandmother joined in my childhood abandonment as the two of us dipped the bread in fresh cream and brown sugar and ate to our heart's content. Life in my grandmother's home was safe, warm, and delicious! All my life I have aspired to emulate it.

An experience like the one I had at my grandmother's house may seem like a practical impossibility today. Gardens are often tended by landscapers. Winter afternoons cuddling together are rare. And most mothers don't have the time or energy for baking bread anymore. Spending precious time with our children may even seem like an indulgence. It is not. It is a priority we need to *make* time for if we want our children to feel loved and secure. Somehow we need to find the time to create an environment that speaks "home" to our children and gives them experiences and memories that they will later cherish as adults.

Creating a home environment for our children doesn't have to mean coming up with special projects to occupy or entertain them. Some of the best memories of home come from doing everyday activities together. Young children especially love to "help," and the opportunities we give them not only create special times for bonding but give them a feeling of accomplishment and responsibility. And even if not much bread is baked at home today, most children can help their parents make (or at least eat!) chocolate chip cookies—the aroma of which will evoke memories of home for the rest of their lives.

Through shared everyday activities as well as the celebrations of important milestones (see Chapter 3, "Creating a Sense of Family"), my husband and I worked to create an environment that all of our children could call home. These days we watch with delight the many ways our grown children are creating a home for their children. One of our daughters-in-law has a small garden where she, like my grandmother, teaches her little girl to plant seeds and harvest pumpkins for Halloween. The intimacy of shared activities creates for children a sense of continuity and security, a feeling of being at home.

A Space for Everyone. With two parents, eight children, and a dog, privacy was sometimes hard to come by in our house. Nevertheless, privacy is an important consideration in creating a home. Even very young children need privacy, a place to be apart, a place to psychologically withdraw. Privacy is especially important in a binuclear family. Space may be limited if the family is large, but everyone needs to be provided with a space over which they have some control, where they can keep the things that they treasure. Even if a child's space consists of only half a bedroom, he or she needs to have a say about who may enter that half bedroom and when.

It is essential that children have a place where they will not be disturbed, a place where they can read, daydream, and pretend. It is in the privacy of their special space that they are free to explore their dreams and discover their self-identity. Both children who feel that their home is being taken over and children who are moving into someone else's house are likely to feel better about their new space if they are given the freedom to personalize it. Painting, rearranging furniture, and buying or making new accessories are relatively simple and inexpensive ways to personalize a child's room as well as being activities that parents and children can enjoy together—even if you do have to do most of the painting! When there isn't time or money for redecorating—which was the case for our family—the children can still make their space their own unique corner of the world by decorating it with posters, bulletin boards, photos, and mementos. I remember pinning up magazine photographs of different dog breeds above my bed at Grandma's house and lying in bed dreaming that one day I would have puppies like that. My dream came true—I have actually managed to own several of those dreamed-of breeds!

Children's dream spaces sometimes extend beyond the house to the surrounding environment. My husband's dream space when he was a child was an old car body discarded in the woods behind his farmhouse. I had a playhouse. It was an old, red, weathered granary that my grandfather had cleaned out for me. I must have spent hundreds of hours in that playhouse, playing a little girl's game of homemaking. I decorated it with old curtains and used wooden boxes for my stove and refrigerator. I made cakes and pies out of mud and decorated them with twigs and red berries from the caragana hedge. I had a splendid time!

Even though we were aware of how important it was, Leonard and I were unable, in the first years of our marriage, to provide our children with spaces of their own. It is unfortunate, but a large family has limitations, and allotting individual space to each child is nearly always impossible. Even so, I saw them create little nests for themselves. It may have been within the narrow confines of a bunk bed or only half of a room that seemed to have an invisible wall down the middle, but they did manage, somehow, to create a space for themselves. Probably, the very best space for each of them was the outdoors, where I can remember seeing them sitting under a tree, on the beach, or in the fishing boat. One son spent nearly all his summers sailing. I think, whatever the constraints, the human spirit longs for and creates dream spaces for itself.

The desire to manipulate our physical environment is a human need that begins in childhood. Giving our children and stepchildren the freedom to create an environment in which they can dream is another way of creating home for them. In their pretending they express their unique identity and discover how to create for themselves the home of their future; in their dreaming they form an image of who they want to be and what wonders their future will hold.

The enjoyment I experienced as a little girl playing home has stayed with me throughout my adult life. I adore making a home: decorating, baking, and doing everything that creates and speaks of home.

Challenges for the Couple. Sharing a home in a binuclear family has ramifications for the couple as well as the children. Even though the newly married couple may be overjoyed with each other, creating a home together will be a huge adjustment. Unlike couples that are in their first marriage and have no children, these couples do not have time alone in which they can settle in with each other. Their new marriage is burdened with anxiety about how their children will adjust to their new living arrangements. Seeing the children's confusion and pain is very unsettling and has the power to detract from the joy the couple experiences in each other.

Whether the husband moves into the wife's home or the wife moves into his home, even the most easygoing man is bound to have some difficulty adjusting. If the man is the one moving in, he may have trouble finding a place in his wife's house that he can call his own. If, on the other hand, his wife moves into his home, he will have to somehow accommodate all her furniture and possessions. She more than likely is quite different than his previous wife and has preferences and values that are unique to her. She may turn the household upside down with a totally different style of managing. He may love his new wife with all his heart, but he is bound to feel at least a small sense of intrusion. And if several children are involved, it could feel like a full-scale invasion! Signs of tension and confusion might break through his normally calm and controlled demeanor. It is a wise wife who recognizes and is sensitive to his process of adjustment.

Meanwhile, the wife is dealing with adjustment issues of her own. If her new husband and his children move into her home, they may upset her way of doing things. And moving into a previous wife's home is an incredible challenge for any woman. It certainly was for me. For whatever the reason, women have, over the years, tended to identify more strongly with their houses than men have. For a woman, in fact, it can be a matter of years—even if she is free to change whatever she wants—before any different house feels like it is *her* home. But particularly if she is moving into the house that her husband and stepchildren already consider home, a new wife needs to be sensitive to the effect that any changes she makes will have on the rest of the family.

For most women, though, the question of "home" goes even deeper than the question of "house." A house cannot be a home unless it creates a warm and loving environment. Women who come from loving, secure childhood homes may have less difficulty adjusting to another home than those whose childhood experience was negative and transient. I have been grateful for the home my grandmother offered me, since the home of my family of origin was fraught with instability and chaos; consequently "home" was an intense issue for me.

My father's alcoholism subjected our family to precarious living circumstances that were for me, as a child, a source of embarrassment and fear. As a youngster my living situation varied from living in a lovely small rental house surrounded with rosebushes to living in a teardrop trailer where we had to use the public bathroom. Is it any wonder that as an adult I was, for a time, obsessed with home? After my divorce I purchased a lovely home that I enjoyed immensely. But in less than two years I remarried. I never anticipated the emotional shock I experienced when I moved into the home that my husband had shared with his first wife. It was beautiful, large, and nearly new, with plenty of room for all of our children. It had a big yard with a hill for them to slide down in the winter. It had been professionally decorated with lovely furniture and accessories. It was by any standard a beautiful home, and I felt like a trespasser!

I did what I could to make Leonard's house my home, but I consciously chose the children as my first priority. Our family was large and there was a lot to do. I had to make three recipes of hot cereal every morning, I had to wash loads of clothes, clean lots of rooms, buy lots of groceries, and go to lots of teacher's conferences. There was simply no time or energy to make big changes. With the exception of moving in a couch and two chairs from my previous house, it was twelve years before we painted or made major decorating changes. It would not have been wise to do so earlier. Our focus needed to be on creating the family that ultimately gave all of us a sense of home.

When I moved into my husband's home I made two major mistakes that unfortunately caused me unnecessary pain and anger.

The first and lesser mistake was to sell my mother's piano. My husband's home had a piano, so rather than go to the trouble of moving my mother's I impulsively sold it. I regretted it immediately! I had beautiful images of Mother playing the piano, and I would have immensely enjoyed the presence of her piano in my home. The second mistake was incredibly stupid. I moved into the bedroom that my husband and his previous wife had shared. In fact I moved into the same bed. At the very least I should have purchased a new bed and linens. I did not feel that the bedroom was my own until fifteen years later when we redid the entire house. The purpose of my writing this book is that I might offer a wee bit of wisdom to new stepmothers. Here it is: Do not sleep in the same bed as the previous wife!

Even though living in another woman's house was painful, my situation was far from grim. God gave me a reprieve: I only had to live in that house part of the time. Immediately after our engagement we heard about a cottage for sale on a small lake thirty-five miles away. My husband acted quickly and fortunately was able to purchase it. He sensed how important it was for all of us to have a new space. It was one of the greatest blessings we could have received. We loved living at the lake. It was a neutral space that, more than any other experience, helped form us as family.

The first few years I lived in my husband's home were paradoxical. I felt very much at home in my husband's love, while at the same time, I felt alien living in the external home in which he had lived with his first wife. Living in what I perceived as another woman's house triggered within me my childhood experience of homelessness. It wasn't until many years later that I was able to feel at home in Leonard's home.

Nurturing "At Homeness" within Our Souls

As we're instructed when we fly, in the event of an emergency we have to put the oxygen mask on ourselves first so that we will be able to help our children. And when we come into a stepfamily, we can't expect to create a feeling of home for our children and stepchildren unless we can first feel a sense of "at homeness" ourselves.

As is so often the case, suffering has a hidden potential for growth. Psychiatrist Rollo May concludes that any event can be a blessing for growth or a curse that can cripple.[3] There was an undeniable gift of growth in my experience of feeling homeless. The anguish of feeling homeless forced me to resolve the issue of homelessness that had been a lifelong source of pain for me. I was an adult, and a wonderful man loved me. I also had eight wonderful children who were depending on me. I was ready, at last, to do what was necessary to be healed of the memories of this painful conflict.

The spirit works in marvelous ways. Just when I was ready the right resources appeared. One of those was a book by Matthew and Dennis Linn titled *Healing Life's Hurts*. It is a marvelous book that contains reflection exercises and prayers that lead people through an integrative process of inner healing. The Linn brothers believe that healing painful memories involves a process similar to that of dying. In *Healing Life's Hurts* they creatively apply Elisabeth Kubler-Ross's five stages of death and dying (denial, anger, bargaining, depression, and acceptance) to people who are processing inner emotional pain.[4]

I was homesick for a home; I probably had always been. I vowed to heal my pain of homelessness, and in my deep desire I persisted through the exercises and ways to pray for healing that the Linn brothers offered.

As I concluded my sometimes-tortuous journey through *Healing Life's Hurts*, I was introduced to the practice of contemplative prayer. It deepened and firmly grounded the healing I experienced in using the prayer exercises. It could not have come at a better time. It led me to my interior home. With enthusiasm I studied the principles of contemplative prayer and gradually developed a daily practice. Contemplative prayer is a prayer of surrender in which we come before God in a silent stance of reverence, emptied of all thoughts, strivings, and distractions. A quiet space and a relaxed, attentive body posture facilitate contemplative prayer.[5] Contemplative prayer is grounded in compassionate love and has a unique capacity for transformation and healing; it brings us *home* to the preciousness of our true selves before God.

In my quest for resolution and healing of my experience of homelessness, I also sought out consolation in nature and, following the ritual of childhood walks with my grandmother, began to walk long distances daily. I made a conscious effort to remain in the present moment, allowing God's creative power in nature to embrace and enliven me. Walking in silent rhythm, emptied of all but the present moment, is similar to contemplative prayer; it is very restorative and transforming.

There are many ways to nurture an "at homeness" within our souls. Cleaning our home, doing the laundry, cooking—the ordinary tasks of daily life—when done in a contemplative, mindful manner, can foster within our hearts a deep sense of belonging, a sense of home. Gunilla Norris, in her book *Being Home*, expresses this idea beautifully: "How then do we come home spiritually and dwell there? In my own life I have found no better way than to value and savor the sacredness of daily living, to rely on repetition, that humdrum rhythm which heals and steadies."[6] What woman among us has not experienced the prayerfulness of a day spent quietly cleaning, experienced pride and harmony at a beautifully ordered home, and in the process of cleaning her home felt ordered within herself?

All these ways led me to resolve the issue of homelessness that had haunted me for so long. Ironically, it was homelessness that welcomed me home. It was homelessness that led me to journey deep within the silence of my own spirit to discover who I was before God, to discover my true home in God's love. It was homelessness that led me to hear clearly the invitation of Jesus: Make your home in me (see John 15:4).

I am finally home.

Deep within the stillness of my heart I can hear God whisper, "Welcome home."

For Your Personal Growth

Exercise 1: Saying Goodbye

Joyce Rupp, in her book *Praying Our Goodbyes*, states that if we are to welcome our new circumstances in life it is essential to say goodbye to our past.[7]

Saying goodbye to her previous home could be very helpful for the remarried woman who is faced with the challenge of making a home for herself and her children in her husband's home. Entering her husband's home may flood her with intense feelings, which could possibly serve as an obstacle in the creation of a new home with her newly combined family. Saying a prayerful goodbye to her previous home has the potential of focusing her energy and gracing her with enthusiasm for the creation of her new home.

The process Rupp suggests for letting go consists of four specific tasks: Recognition, Reflection, Ritualization, and Reorientation. For the remarried woman entering her husband's home, her transition might look like this:

1. Recognition:

What losses do you experience? Do you experience a loss of privacy, personal expression, and control? Do you miss the intimacy of sharing your past home with only your own children? Do you miss your old neighborhood, or your friends that lived nearby? Do you miss your yard, certain trees, your garden or flowers? What emotional pain do you experience at that loss? Are you angry, sad, resigned?

It may be painful, but it is important to be truthful with yourself and identify any losses you may be experiencing.

2. Reflection:

Take time to reflect quietly on the losses you have identified. Sit silently with them. Take them before God, who loves you. Tell God how you feel. Be silent and allow God to reveal your deeper feelings to you. As you return, again and again, to prayerfully be with God in your losses, you will hear God's gentle whisper of hope and encouragement. You may hear it in Scripture, in nature, or through remembrance of a song or a letter from a friend. Slowly your reflection time will give you insight, hope, peace, and acceptance.

3. Ritualization:

Rupp states that ritualization of our goodbyes is an important step that includes "the use of images or symbols and some kind of movement in our prayer."[8]

What are the images or symbols that speak to you of the loss of your home, saying goodbye to it, and saying hello to your new home with your combined family? Search deeply within yourself for that image. Could it be an empty nest and the symbol of a bird gathering sticks to create a new nest? Might it be a train on a journey from one place to the next? Could it be the image of an uprooted tree and the planting of a new tree? Could it be a butterfly emerging from its chrysalis into new life?

After arriving at the image, think of a way of praying your good-bye and hello through movement and physical action. You might transplant a special perennial from your previous home into the yard of your new home. You might light a candle, plant a tree, or build a nest to which you periodically add new strings, twigs, etc. With your husband and children and stepchildren you might have a celebration of blessing your new home. Create a ritual of your goodbye and hello.

4. Reorientation:

The reflection and ritualization of the loss of your previous home can give you the courage to go forward and create a new home for your combined family. Insight and a sense of meaning are gained through reflection and ritual, through connecting our pain with God, who heals us. This new meaning reorients our energy and focus; it restores our trust and graces our path in the creation of a new home that is welcoming and nurturing for the entire family.[9] Make a plan of what your ideal combined family home would be like.

Exercise 2: Blessing Your Home

Use the following blessing as a family prayer to celebrate your home. Let the family gather in a circle, perhaps around the dinner table. Each member can read a different part of the blessing, reserving the first lines for the mother and the final verse for the father.

Blessing of a Home

Loving and gracious God,
We come before you as a newly combined family, born of the love of our mother and father.
We ask you to bless this home we are to share.
May our home be a safe refuge.
Let peace flow within and trouble find no entry.
Within the strength of its walls may we be held safe and secure.
May all of creation permeate our home and grace it with life.
Let trees shelter us with shade and privacy.
May flowers and plants inspire us with their beauty.
May our home provide food for our lives.
Let our meals be prepared with love and eaten with thankfulness.
May the conversation and sharing of our mealtimes nurture our spirits.
May our home be a home of calm serenity.
Let it be an orderly home, one that will provide us with an environment free of chaos.
May it be a haven where we will have the freedom and leisure to study and discover.

Loving God,
May our home be a home of kindness.
As we grow into being a family may love and gentleness be our guides.

Open our hearts that we may be filled with compassion and forgiveness.
May our home be a home of encouragement and trust.
Let our cares and anxieties be lovingly heard and answered.
May the opinions and ideas of all, even the very youngest, be respected.
Lord, enfold our home in your love.
May friendship and hospitality grace its door.
Let all who enter feel your warmth and welcome.
May our home be a home of prayer,
Where individually and together we seek your presence.
May your wisdom lead us into being the person, the family, you most desire us to be.
May our home be a home of celebration,
Let all our holidays, birthdays, and special occasions be wonderful, happy events.
May we always affirm and celebrate the unique gift each member brings to our family.

Gracious and loving God,
Bless this house.
May your angels guard its corners.
May your kindness fill its halls.
May your strength shield it from harm.
Within its rooms may each member of this new family be welcomed home.

Scripture:

1. There will be times when you, as a stepmother, will feel that you have wandered into a foreign land where you know neither the customs nor the language of the family you have entered. You may even feel that you have lost the place of serenity within your own heart. At these times take consolation from the words God

addressed to the people of Judah when they were exiled in Babylon, a thousand miles from home:

Thus says the LORD *of hosts, the God of Israel, to all the exiles whom I have sent into exile from Jerusalem to Babylon: Build houses and live in them; plant gardens and eat what they produce. . . . But seek the welfare of the city where I have sent you into exile, and pray to the* LORD *on its behalf, for in its welfare you will find your welfare. . . . For surely I know the plans I have for you, says the* LORD, *plans for your welfare and not for harm, to give you a future with hope.* (Jeremiah 29:4-5, 7, 11)

2. Listen to Christ say to you:

Make your home in me as I make mine in you. (John 15:4, paraphrased)

During your personal solitary prayer time say these words over and over, slowly and aloud, each time emphasizing a different word. Let these words of Christ accompany you throughout the day like the refrain of a song.

NOTES

1. Clare Cooper Marcus, *House as a Mirror of Self: Exploring the Deeper Meaning of Home* (Berkeley: Conari Press, 1997), 8.

2. Marcus, 151.

3. Rollo May, *The Art of Counseling* (Nashville: Abingdon, 1967), 35.

4. Dennis Linn and Matthew Linn, *Healing Life's Hurts: Healing Memories through the Five Stages of Forgiveness* (New York: Paulist Press, 1978), 11.

5. Some masters of contemplative prayer emphasize attentiveness to breathing, while others use counting or the repetition of a particular word or sound to quiet and still the body and mind. There are many ways one might pray contemplatively; masters of contemplative prayer approach it in different ways, emphasizing different aspects or methods. In the 1970s Thomas Keating, a Cistercian monk at St. Benedict's Monastery in Snowmass, Colorado, formed Contemplative Outreach, a lay ministry group whose mission is to teach contemplative prayer. They have developed centering prayer as an excellent, yet simple, way of introducing one to contemplative prayer. Contemplative Outreach has been extremely successful and has enriched the spiritual life of thousands. Contemplative prayer is, first and foremost—whatever way you choose to practice it—a resting in God's love.

6. Gunilla Norris, *Being Home: Discovering the Spiritual in the Everyday* (Mahwah, N.J.: Hidden Spring, 2001), xiii.

7. Joyce Rupp, *Praying Our Goodbyes* (Notre Dame, In.: Ava Maria Press, 1988).

8. Rupp, 87.

9. Rupp, 83–95.

CHAPTER 3

Creating a Sense of Family

Deep within every heart lies a yearning for family. We hunger to belong, to feel safe. All of us, whether we are young or old, need a nurturing and stable environment in which we can feel free to discover and express our uniqueness.

A newly created stepfamily is usually suffering from many emotional wounds. At the heart of this pain is a loss of identity, a crisis of esteem and stability. Initially the entire family, adults and children, reel with confusion and anxiety. The children, of course, are especially vulnerable. They have been deeply hurt by the devastating effects of the dismantlement of their family of origin. Their young minds and spirits cannot comprehend the changes; they are not able to envision a future in which they can trust and feel safe.

Fortunately, however, families are invested with a wonderful power to heal. Within the womb of a nurturing family, children can learn again to trust; they can gradually grow in an awareness of who they are and how special they are. Slowly they can begin to develop a sense of belonging and of being cherished. Through the energy of the love they share, a couple with determination and a sincere desire can bring about this healing as they create and live out their own family traditions and rituals.

As I look back on how we struggled to create a sense of family, I have a keener appreciation of family customs and rituals such as holidays and birthdays, along with annual events like family vacations. I am aware more than ever of how powerful all these things are in creating a feeling of identity and belonging within a family and in creating the kind of sheer joy that can bridge many heartaches and struggles along the way.

The Power of Ritual

From the dawn of human history, we have celebrated significant moments in our lives through ritual actions, songs, and meals. The rituals that mark family gatherings and celebrations are powerful. Rituals employ symbols, engage all our senses, and evoke memories and emotions. Rituals tap the wellsprings of our total personality. As families we need rituals to discover, maintain, and renew our connection to the values that give meaning to our life together. Rituals invite us to cherish ordinary human events and actions in an extraordinary, yet simple, way.

For a stepfamily, the rituals of celebration and gathering are especially important. Human beings, and children in particular, need a sense of structure in their lives in order to feel secure. For children in stepfamilies, that structure needs to be rebuilt, since it was dismantled by the death of or separation from a parent. Because of their symbolism and repetitive nature, rituals have the unique capacity to help rebuild that sense of order by conveying the security, continuity, love, and healing that stepfamilies need. Family rituals can inspire hope and a sense of oneness in the newly formed stepfamily.

The symbols of ritual, such as candles, gifts, food, music, scent, textures, and touch are simple yet mysteriously powerful. Through their mere repetition they have the ability to evoke the warm memories and feelings associated with shared family moments. As an illustration we need only to recall the feelings from our own childhood as we prepared to blow out the candles on our cake while our family and friends sang "Happy Birthday." And who among us doesn't have a gift from childhood that we still cherish, that still warms our hearts with the memory of the loved one who gave it to us?

Parties to celebrate accomplishments such as graduations create affirming memories as they convey a family's love and "celebration" of one another. But family rituals don't have to be parties in order to create memories that will endure. For instance, our new stepfamily frequently had our Sunday supper of pizza and milkshakes in front of the fireplace. The children still speak of those happy times. On the last day of school, we always celebrated by going to the ice cream stand for banana splits. Now some of our children do that with their children. Quite simple, but how enduring—and endearing!

The sacraments of initiation—baptism, first Eucharist, and confirmation—impart a special significance in creating a sense of family. These sacraments affirm our membership in the larger family of the church. They speak to us of God's continuing love and faithfulness; they connect us to our source of life and being; they uniquely bond us with each other.

The events of my own first Communion and confirmation have nurtured me my entire life, and their treasured memory continues to provide me with a sense of confidence and mission. I am grateful to my mother for her loving effort to make each of those hallmarks of my childhood memorable. I still have the small white satin first Communion dress she hand sewed for me from her wedding suit. For my confirmation, even though we didn't have much money, Mother bought me a lovely dress of white pique and had my picture taken by a professional photographer. And I will never forget the wreath of roses she made for me to wear. Although the full meaning and mystery of those sacraments probably eluded me at the time, the significance of the events did not escape me. My mother's reverential attitude toward my first Communion and confirmation forever impressed upon me her love of God and her love for me.

I attempted to extend this love to my children and stepchildren through our celebration of the sacraments in our new stepfamily. I made every effort to make the day of their celebrations of First Communion and confirmation memorable. We shopped for new clothes, took pictures, and had special family meals. My efforts were motivated by my desire to convey to them that their reception of the sacraments was a very significant event that marked their entry into a deeper relationship of love with God.

Family Celebrations

Although both parents are equally capable of celebrating family events, the responsibility of planning those celebrations has—for whatever reason—traditionally been taken on by the woman. So as stepmothers, even though we are newcomers to the family, we can expect to be primarily in charge of family celebrations and special events! This can require a huge expenditure of resources, energy, and time. Yet, we cannot choose a better priority than that of spending our time and energy marking significant family events.

Planning celebrations in a stepfamily requires astute sensitivity. Each subgroup has come to the new family with past traditions and preferences as well as a heightened need for affirmation. While the newly created family needs to discover its own particular spirit of celebration and tradition, an effort must also be directed toward incorporating rituals and practices that the children love and are familiar with from their previous family. It could be quite a scene, for instance, if a child who is accustomed to getting a stocking on Christmas morning does not receive one. To adults a Christmas stocking is just a sock of stuff; to a child it may evoke memories of home.

Our first celebration as a combined family was Christmas. It arrived twenty-five days after our wedding, and it was nearly a disaster.

During those twenty-five days, my three sons and I moved into Leonard's home, and Leonard and I began, as gently as possible, the process of making a home for our combined family. We shifted children from bedroom to bedroom and did various organizing and cleaning tasks, while at the same time we prepared for Christmas. We put up a tree, baked cookies, and tried to do the traditional things that would make our first Christmas memorable. It was an exciting time, filled with hope. Leonard and I were ecstatically in love with each other, and each of us was totally committed to our new life, to our new family, and to loving each other's children. Our experience was brand new, and the thrill of it kept at bay the difficult adjustments we were to eventually face.

Our gift-giving to the children is probably our most vivid memory of that first Christmas and has been a hilarious story that we have enjoyed sharing over the years. As soon as the wedding date was set, anxiety set in. Our first concern was to provide a happy Christmas for the children. The tradition of Christmas had been special for both of our previous families, and Leonard and I felt it was essential that this first Christmas together be wonderful. We knew that the gifts we would give would be important; they did not have to be spectacular, but we wanted to give the children something they really wanted, something that would thrill them.

The problem was that we didn't have time to shop. We were busy selling my house, packing, and buying some necessary bedroom furniture. We had so much to do! We decided to order all the gifts. That way we could get just the right things, and we wouldn't have to spend so much time shopping. We ordered fishing rods and tackle boxes for each of the five boys, and for the three girls we ordered radios and stuffed animals. We did our ordering the last week in October.

Nothing had arrived by the first week in December, so Leonard called the catalog company and inquired. They reassured him that everything was coming. Another week went by and nothing arrived, so he called again and again was comfortably reassured; everything had been sent. Finally, Christmas week came, and still we had nothing. Our confidence in the catalog company was now seriously in question. Leonard placed a desperate call! On the twenty-third of December we received fifteen rods and reels, fifteen tackle boxes, nine radios, and nine stuffed animals! Christmas had arrived in triplicate!

Sometime during Christmas week we had our first family photograph taken. I can barely recognize myself in the picture; I look so harried and confused. We are all there—all ten of us, together with Samantha, our husky. It is impossible to look at that first family portrait and not see tentativeness, confusion, and anxiety; yet we were smiling.

Our Christmas celebration was the first of many family memories we treasured throughout the years. In retrospect, I think of our family celebrations and rituals as being even more precious than they were at the time and wish we had made more effort, been more creative, and just done more. I do think, however, that with our circumstances and the constraints of so many children, we did remarkably well. What is most important is that we managed to preserve the children's expectations of family traditions while at the same time creating memories that would eventually cement the bond of our new family.

I am always amazed that, although the children often appeared unappreciative at the time, they later came to treasure the memory of our family rituals. Now that they are grown they often share how meaningful those celebrations were for them, and some have even emulated our traditions in their own families. Creating beautiful family rituals is worth every effort one must make. Even if their effect is not immediately apparent, they are powerful symbols that have the potential for creating cherished legacies for future generations.

Family Vacations

Family vacations create the kinds of lasting memories that contribute to a sense of family in addition to providing educational opportunities to explore new places and learn new skills. Throughout the years I often felt envious of families who went on marvelous vacations. The expense and logistics of a vacation for a family the size of ours made it almost impossible. We managed it only twice. The children have wonderful memories of both of those trips and still talk about the time, during Christmas week, when we went to see *The Nutcracker* in Minneapolis. Talk about differences in perspective—I remember the whole experience as a nightmare! Taking eight children, five of whom were teenagers, to a hotel for several days stretched our patience, to say the least. I promised myself never to do it again!

We may not have been able to take trips to faraway and exciting places, but we were far from deprived. Shortly after our marriage we purchased a lake home, where we lived during the summer months. The children became water rats, spending every possible moment in the lake. Every evening Leonard pulled them on water skis until it grew so dark that he could no longer see to drive the boat. Encouraged by the older ones, even the most timid of the children became excellent skiers. We had a small sailboat, and they taught themselves and each other the rudiments of wind and tack. They played badminton until the lawn was completely annihilated, keeping a running account of who was the current champion. They also learned how to fish, and one of my favorite memories is the image of one of them contemplatively silhouetted against the setting sun, rod in hand.

Our summers at the lake were a great gift to us. There we were in our own world, embraced by the trees and the water, soothed and comforted by the quieting sounds of nature. Away from the influences of peers and free to play and laugh together, we were all helped to shed our inhibitions and shyness. Much of our bonding and identity as a family took place in our summers at the lake. Serendipitously, the lake that we lived on was named Union Lake.

As a combined family we are grateful for our lake summers, and we are aware that not all families are that fortunate. There are, however, many ways to immerse oneself and one's family in nature and to glean its enrichment and healing. All our young adults love the outdoors and have discovered many ways of enjoying it. Some with families are involved with camping and love it, occasionally joining with other families to share an excursion. Sports and the activities that surround them have been a lot of fun for most of our young families. One of our grown sons, who is divorced, spends hours on the golf course with his young son, walking the fairways, seeing the sunset, and watching the seasons unfold. Nature seems to beckon all of them; some like to canoe, others prefer to snowmobile. They all seem, however, in some way to be nature bound, and whatever their circumstances they find a way to enjoy it.

Accepting the Reality

No matter how carefully we plan, something invariably seems to happen to disrupt our idyllic family times and celebrations. It might be as small an incident as a burned turkey or as serious as the eruption of a destructive behavior such as substance abuse. Holidays are particularly vulnerable to emotional outbursts, since expectations and sentimentality are unreasonably high. At Christmastime, in particular, the pressure is intense for the gilded ideal. Not every family knows the peace of a silent night. The contrast between the ideal and reality can be jarring for most families; for stepfamilies it can be traumatic.

One of the most disruptive and stressful experiences for binuclear families occurs when a child or children must visit their noncustodial or joint-custodial parent. Holiday scheduling around visitations can be difficult. Visitation time can be extremely unsettling, yet it is essential that the children spend quality time with their noncustodial parent.

I never coped well with the stress of the visitations. My sons were shuffled between their father and me once or twice a month. I know they also struggled with feelings that were difficult: "Where do I belong? Who is this new dad, and how do I please him? If I love him, am I being disloyal to my own dad?" I only made matters worse. When I took them to visit their father, hard as I tried I was never able to part from them without tears. The visitations went on for over twelve years, and I really do not remember a single time when I didn't cry. It was not that I did not trust their father; it simply saddened me to part with them. As the years went by, the visitations became less painful, but they always remained a struggle for me. I would like to be able to say that I had been stronger, had been better adjusted, or had managed it all cheerfully. The truth, however, is that I hadn't.

Family celebrations such as graduations, First Communions, and confirmations can also be occasions of stress. Noncustodial and joint-custodial parents have every right to be at such events, and it is essential for the children that they are. It can, however, prove to be extremely awkward and even embarrassing.

Reality reigns. Nothing is idyllic. Relationships in a stepfamily are complex, and frequently there are issues of loyalty, resentment, and competitiveness. For instance, sibling rivalry between children and stepchildren is not uncommon; nor is territorial behavior or jealousy. Relationship conflicts can be very unsettling in a stepfamily and cause a stepparent to feel ill prepared, confused, and overwhelmed. Unfortunately, there are no easy answers. Each situation must be lived through with the greatest measure of graciousness we can muster. We must forgive others and ourselves when, through our pain and limitations, we simply do not rise to the occasion. We are, after all, human, and it is in the acceptance of our human limitations and sufferings that we grow into holiness.

The words attributed to Flannery O'Connor speak to our experience:

"It is not a struggle to submit but a struggle to accept and with passion. I mean possibly with joy."

For Your Personal Growth

Exercises:
1. In order to be creative and sensitive in preparing family celebrations and rituals, recall what was precious to you as a child.

2. Create a situation in which the children feel safe to share memories of previous celebrations and ideas for celebrating.

Scripture:
Hold in your heart the prayer St. Paul offers for all families:

I bow my knees before the Father, from whom every family in heaven and on earth takes its name. I pray that, according to the riches of his glory, he may grant that you may be strengthened in your inner being with power through his Spirit, and that Christ may dwell in your hearts through faith, as you are being rooted and grounded in love. I pray that you may have the power to comprehend, with all the saints, what is the breadth and length and height and depth, and to know the love of Christ that surpasses knowledge, so that you may be filled with all the fullness of God. Now to him who by the power at work within us is able to accomplish abundantly far more than all we can ask or imagine, to him be glory in the church and in Christ Jesus to all generations, forever and ever. Amen. (Ephesians 3:14-21)

Growing as a Stepmom—with God's Help!

CHAPTER 4

Love Heals

Everyone comes into the stepfamily with a "broken heart." The members of the newly formed stepfamily are grieving.

The adults are grieving the end of a dream, the end of a marriage either by death or divorce. The children are grieving the loss of a parent through death or the loss of the daily presence of a parent through divorce. In either case, the children have lost their family of origin.

If the stepmother or stepfather in the newly formed stepfamily had never been married or never had children, there could possibly be one less grieving adult. Ironically, he or she may be grieving the fact that they have no children of their own. Regardless of how many are grieving, the newly formed stepfamily is experiencing the chaos and confusion of loss and change.

The degree of grieving can vary greatly. If, for instance, a considerable amount of time has elapsed between the loss and remarriage, some resolution of grief may have occurred. One of the most frequent mistakes couples make is to marry too soon after a divorce or death. When Leonard and I married sixteen months after the death of his first wife, we had no idea what the effect would be on his children. One of my stepchildren later shared with me, "You and Dad didn't give us a chance to adjust. It was good for you that you married quickly, but not for us." She was absolutely right! Studies show that children whose parents date and remarry within two years following a death feel unsafe and experience more emotional problems than children whose parents marry later. After the two-year period, most children were eager to see their parent remarried and were less disturbed emotionally.[1] I suspect this is also true for children of divorce.

If a family has the benefit of professional counseling, or if they have a strong extended family to console and support them through their crisis, they should have significantly less grief upon entering the new stepfamily. Maturity, coping skills, and depth of religious faith also affect an individual's ability to resolve grief. Many other factors influence the degree of grief and brokenness that the newly formed stepfamily experiences. The most important thing to remember is that, in the heart of each member, there exists a tender vulnerability that cries out for safety, stability, and love.

Helping Our Children Heal After Divorce

Each year close to a million children in the United States see their parents divorce.[2] That is a lot of vulnerability! That is a huge number of confused and frightened children, not to mention an enormous number of parents who are attempting to build a new life for themselves and their children.

We love our children, and we see their suffering as a result of our divorce. How are we to help them? The myth that if the parents are happier, the children will be happier is dispelled by Judith Wallerstein and her associates in their research report, *The Unexpected Legacy of Divorce*. Their twenty-five year study has led them to believe that parents who divorce make assumptions and decisions according to their own adult agenda without enough consideration of their children. They assert that divorcing adults cannot fathom how overwhelmed their children are and cannot imagine the depth of their feelings and thoughts. Wallerstein cites national studies showing that children from divorced and remarried families experience more depression, learning problems, and social malad-justments such as aggression, early sexual behavior, and substance abuse. There is a higher rate of divorce among children of divorce; they experience more illness, and they are two to three times more likely to require psychological counseling.[3] Those are grim statis-tics! It is imperative that we do all we possibly can to help our children traverse this treacherous path.

It is our responsibility as parents to help our children cope with the anxiety of a divorce. All too frequently, though, parent-ing suffers when parents divorce. The newly divorced parents are often overwhelmed by their own feelings of grief and preoccupied with the stress of creating a new life for themselves. Yet their chil-dren—who are also grieving—need them more than ever. Without patience, love, and understanding, children of divorce are at risk of suffering lifelong detrimental effects.

Our goal is to restructure for our children a family that offers them stability and love. Children have a right to know the reasons the divorce occurred. It is essential that even the youngest of chil-dren have somewhat of an understanding of why the divorce hap-pened. Parents should share with their children the sorrow, inner struggle, and reluctance they experienced when they decided to divorce as well as the fact that they will never get back together. A conversation addressing these issues is valuable, and can be geared to the different developmental ages of the children.

The style of parenting that divorced parents develop can sig-nificantly influence the adjustment of their children. Studies have shown that children whose parents are consistent and adopt a lov-ing, supportive style of parenting adjust better and are less stressed than those children whose parents adopted a permissive or rigidly authoritarian style or were disengaged and neglectful.[4]

Understanding children's feelings is essential if we are to help them cope with the trauma of divorce. Sometimes children feel that they are in some way to blame for their parents' divorce. They may think that if they had been better children, then the divorce would not have happened. An age-appropriate explanation of the reasons for the divorce can alleviate them of imagined guilt.

Children of divorce also suffer from a lack of closure, making divorce sometimes more difficult to adjust to than the death of a parent. For the children whose parent has died and are old enough to understand, there is an obvious permanence and irreversibility. The children of a divorce, however, often entertain the fantasy of the reunion of their parents. Yet until these children understand and accept the permanence of the divorce, they cannot begin to adjust to it.[5]

Lack of closure is also evident in the sometimes excruciating matters of custody and visitation rights. Divorce can be a nightmare that never seems to end! Anger and conflict between the divorced parents cause immeasurable damage to their children. The children experience great stress, and their loyalty is in conflict—they are torn between their parents. I find it alarming that studies show that even six years after divorce, 20–25 percent of couples are still engaged in combative behavior. They "make nasty comments about each other, seek to undermine each other's relationship with the child, and fight openly in front of the child."[6] Hostility toward the other parent can be very damaging, and ironically it often causes resentment toward the parent who is speaking negatively.

Parents are the adults in the relationship, and hence they have a responsibility to work out custody and visitation arrangements without causing their children additional stress. It is essential for their well-being that children maintain a good relationship with both parents. Thus, no matter how difficult it may be, parents must reach a cooperative co-parenting agreement in which they can be supportive of each other's efforts for the benefit of their children.

Time with the noncustodial parent is crucial to the adjustment of the children of divorce. In most divorces the father is the non-custodial parent. Studies have continually found that children who have close relationships with their fathers after a divorce adjust much better than children who do not. Cognitively and socially they are more developed than children whose fathers were passive. It is not an easy task to be a part-time parent. I have always felt grateful for the continuing love and care the father of my children extended to them. When I asked one of my sons what aspect of the divorce was most difficult for him, he said, "It was always going back and forth. There never was enough time with Dad. We just got started and we had to leave."

It is a wise parent who is compassionate toward the noncustodial parent's situation and works to foster their children's relationship with him or her.

Helping children make a healthy adjustment to their parents' divorce affects them not only when they are young, but when they are forming relationships as adults, as well. Children of divorce have a tendency to see their parents' divorce as a failure. Fear of repeating their parents' mistakes, combined with their fear of rejection and a lack of confidence, make them wary of commitment. In their determination not to fail, they may construct many obstacles to the development of a satisfying and enriching relationship. Parents' consistent nurturing of their children's self-image throughout the years can go a long way toward building the confidence, trust, and courage needed to extend and commit in a relationship. Seeing their parents in new marriages that are life giving also helps by showing children that marriages can and do work. Finally, for children of divorce who find themselves alone and lonely in adulthood, psychological counseling may prove beneficial. Their loneliness may be a legacy of their parents' divorce.

And what about my own sons? Did they bring grief to the stepfamily? Of course they did. They had lost their nuclear family, were separated from their father, and were taken away from their home and friends. They went through many difficult times, and my heart ached for them. I wish that I had been more sensitive to their needs at the time and that I had been more available to them. To their credit, I can say, thirty-two years later, that they are wonderful young men—mature, responsible, and competent. All three are currently in loving marriages. As any mother worth her salt would say, "They are terrific!"

Helping Ourselves Heal After Divorce

Divorce creates major upheaval, and those involved must gather all the resources possible to make a good recovery. Initial postdivorce feelings of guilt, anger, depression, and emotional instability are common. Friendships and social relationships are altered. Quite often there is financial difficulty. A woman may have to return to a profession from which she has been absent for a number of years. A woman unskilled in the work world and facing poverty may have to return to school. Ultimately, she may not be able to depend on her former husband to support her. He may have difficulty paying child support and/or alimony when at the same time he is attempting to create a new life for himself, perhaps in a new family. Children experience great chaos and, more than ever, need a loving, consistent parent. There is so much to deal with!

The result of these factors is increased stress, which brings with it a greater vulnerability to illness. And with all the new challenges that accompany divorce, the last thing anyone needs is to get sick! It is essential that the newly divorced do everything they can to take care of themselves by eating well and exercising. Our efforts to take care of ourselves and to attempt to relieve stress are rewarded with an increased sense of confidence and well-being.

E. Mavis Hetherington and John Kelly have conducted extensive research on divorce. Their work, *For Better or for Worse: Divorce Reconsidered*, published in 2002, presents their study of 1,400 divorced families, which they followed for nearly thirty-two years. They "confirm, resoundingly, that the end of marriage is usually brutally painful," but they also see divorce as providing an opportunity for life-transforming personal growth, particularly for women.[7] That was true in my case, but it was a long, lonely struggle, reaching back into my childhood.

I grew up in a dysfunctional family. My father was an alcoholic, and my mother was depressed most of the time. My mother and father divorced when I was in college, but my mother couldn't sustain the shame and guilt of divorcing my father, and she remarried him in less than a year. In college I met an older student upon whom I became dependent. It was not a healthy relationship, and although I was urged to end it, I married him. He was a good man, but we had both come into the marriage with serious unresolved issues. And although we tried, we could not resolve our differences. After twelve years and three children, and braced by my childhood experience, I filed for divorce.

The months following the divorce were rough. I was reeling from the problems in my marriage, the emotional strain of the divorce proceedings, and the effect that it was all having on my children. I experienced a serious health setback and needed two surgeries for a condition that is often exacerbated by stress. I went back to school for two years to become certified as a nurse anesthetist. I was fortunate to be able to buy a house. With the help of family, friends, and counselors, I was also able to begin to heal.

Friends and the supportive network they offer can be of great help in recovery. It is not easy in the midst of new demands to find the time to nurture friendships, but it is essential to be receptive and make the effort. And, as for therapy, I wouldn't have survived without it!

But what sustained me most through my divorce and the years that followed was my interior life of faith. A spiritual director can be a great help in supporting you in your relationship with God. This may be a new idea for some, but I can assure you it is a worthwhile consideration. Spiritual directors don't provide the answers to all our questions; rather, they lead us toward our own truth and resolutions.

A tremendous blessing that aided my recovery was the fact that the church annulled my first marriage. It happened in a crazy way. A stranger approached me after Mass one day and suggested I call a priest who directed the Marriage Tribunal for our diocese. I was amazed to learn that this priest knew me and knew of my situation. I met with him, and he was encouraging. Two years later, my annulment was granted. I felt as if God had put a hand on my shoulder and said, "It's okay." The annulment was a great gift that allowed me to remarry in the church I love.[8]

In their study, Hetherington and Kelly conclude that divorce leads some people to develop abilities and skills they might not otherwise have acquired. The necessity of managing on their own prompts many people—women, in particular—to assert a degree of independence and self-reliance that they may never even have known they had. That was definitely true for me. After the divorce, it was sink or swim! Thank goodness, there were many people who helped me stay afloat. I have been extremely fortunate to have many people who have, throughout my life, taken me under their wing, people who have counseled, mentored, and guided me. I am forever grateful to them.

Although I felt healed in many ways, I did bring grief to my new stepfamily. I still had a way to go to recover from the divorce as well as to continue to deal with the painful emotions from my childhood. I don't know that my recovery will ever be complete. I suspect there will always be a residue from my past that I will need to deal with, a remnant that demands growth.

The adults and children who suffer divorce can go on to lead happy and productive lives. Hetherington and Kelly concluded in their thirty-year study that "it isn't a matter of whether the glass is half empty or half full. In the long run, after a divorce, the glass is three-quarters full of reasonably happy and competent adults and children who have been resilient in coping with the challenges of divorce."[9] At each transition along the way, choices are made. The most important choices are those involving intimate relationships. If these choices and decisions are made with integrity, sensitivity, and care, "the final destination will be one of resiliency, enhancement, and happiness."[10]

Healing After the Death of a Parent

The death of a parent or spouse is one of the most traumatic and stressful events that can occur in a person's life. Yet many of the members of newly formed stepfamilies are still attempting to deal with this grief at the same time that their family dynamic is changing. How we as stepmothers respond to those feelings will have a tremendous impact on the well-being of our new family.

My five stepchildren lost their mother to lung cancer. Less than a year-and-a-half later, their father and I married and my three sons and I moved into their home. Were my stepchildren grieving? Absolutely!

I cringe now at my lack of awareness of their grief. Thirty years ago we were naive about grief and how to cope with it. During the last few years many studies have been conducted that look at how children respond to the death of a parent. These studies can help us identify and meet the needs of a grieving child as well as help us recognize when they may be at risk for emotional problems.

In his book *Children and Grief: When a Parent Dies*, J. William Worden observes that "the death of a parent is one of the most fundamental losses a child can face. . . . [T]he loss of a parent to death and its consequences in the home and in the family change the very core of the child's existence."[11]

Worden stresses that the child's response is strongly influenced by the response of the surviving parent. Seeing the surviving parent cope with his or her grief without being overwhelmed facilitates the child's adjustment. How well the surviving parent is able to parent, and in particular, the parent's emotional and physical availability to the child, directly affects the child's adjustment to loss. But if the surviving parent is severely depressed and unable to function, the child is at risk.

Studies show that the death of a mother is usually more difficult for children than that of a father, since the mother most often assumes the role of emotional caretaker in a family as well as responsibility for the daily routine of the household. Her death results in major disruptions of a child's life. Grief is an ongoing life process. The death of a mother continues to be experienced not only

at the time of her death but also at major events such as gradua-
tion, marriage, and the birth of a first child. A time of crisis can also
precipitate grief. My mother died when I was twenty-nine, and at
sixty-six, I still experience times when my heart cries within me, "I
want my mother." In her book *Motherless Daughters: The Legacy
of Loss*, Hope Edelman shares the poignant stories of daughters
who lost their mothers and how their lives were profoundly altered
by their loss. Their stories speak of the ongoing journey of grief.[12]

Children can respond to the death of their parent in very different ways. Some may have an intense emotional reaction and feel
overwhelmed with sadness and confusion. Others may experience
shock and become numb and withdrawn. Some children feel the
pressure to be very good, not to cry, or to be strong for the surviving parent. Where anger is the dominant emotion, the child may act
out in destructive behavior.

The intensity of the emotions children experience following the
death of a parent can be overwhelming. They need our help in dealing with these emotions. We can start by giving them opportunities
to express their feelings; then we can listen carefully and compas-
sionately without minimizing any of their concerns. We can reas-
sure them that they were not to blame for their parent's death and
that they are safe and loved.

When destructive behaviors result, they are usually short lived.
There are, however, certain behaviors that, when they are of a sustained duration, should be seen as red flags for intervention. These
behaviors include persistent difficulty talking about the dead parent; aggressive behavior; anxious and clinging behavior; persistent
somatic complaints such as headaches and stomachaches; sleeping
difficulties; eating disturbances; marked social withdrawal; school
difficulties or serious academic reversal; persistent self-blame or

guilt; and self-destructive behaviors or expressing a wish to die.[13] These behaviors can also serve to alert us in regard to the children of divorce.

The way children remember their parent's death plays an important role in their ability to deal with their grief. Children need to be able to remember and to memorialize the lost parent not only after the death but throughout their lives. Shared reminiscences can be of help to the child's adjustment.

Being present at and sharing in the ritual surrounding the funeral of a parent can be beneficial even for young children. Just as for adults, attending the funeral can contribute to a sense of closure. Including children in the process can help them accept the reality of their parent's death and lessen feelings that the parent has just vanished, while unnecessarily excluding them may result in feelings of confusion, abandonment, and insecurity. How children are prepared for and participate in the funeral of their parent is crucial. The rituals may be remembered as incredibly beautiful, or the memory of them may be riddled with pain and confusion. Whatever their experience, it is one that will be with them the rest of their lives.

It is worthwhile to consider asking our stepchildren to share with us their experiences surrounding the death and funeral of their parent. This sharing may help alleviate any painful memories that burden them. It can also reinforce good memories and facilitate their connection to the lost parent. I have been told that the funeral of my stepchildren's mother was large and that there were many flowers. Some of the children may have enjoyed sharing this with me, telling me how many friends their mother had, and how beautiful the flowers were. Some may have had unpleasant or painful memories that would have been helpful to vent. One of the greatest gifts a stepmother can give to her grieving stepchild is active and careful listening.

It is not easy to resolve the feelings of emptiness and insecurity that accompany the death of a parent. Maxine Harris, in her book *The Loss That Is Forever*, speaks of the absolute catastrophe and profound emptiness that children experience when a parent dies. Harris stresses the need for the children to stay in touch, to develop an ongoing relationship with the parent. They must renegotiate the meaning of the loss rather than let go of the deceased.[14] Children can maintain a connection with the deceased parent through conversation, pictures, special items, and places. A stepmother can be helpful in maintaining such connections.

We can encourage our stepchildren to talk about their dead parent and to ask questions of extended family members and friends. I love asking my elderly aunts about my mother and father. I love hearing how intelligent and beautiful my mother was and what a good mechanic my dad was. I love telling people how well Mother played the piano without ever having had a lesson and how Daddy taught me to dance. I was an adult when my parents died, and I still find it comforting to talk about them. I can only imagine the comfort it might be for a young or adolescent child. My stepchildren's mother was a talented, bright, beautiful woman. I think it would be delightful for her children to brag about her! Yet my stepchildren spoke very little about their mother. I don't think they were comfortable speaking of her. Perhaps they felt that the subject was off limits, or maybe they were afraid I would react negatively. I am not sure of the reason, but I am sorry that I did not encourage them to talk about her more frequently.

Talking about the deceased parent can be particularly helpful if the child experienced an ambivalent relationship with the parent. Verbalizing feelings can serve to release anger or guilt that burden a child as well as to help clarify and gain understanding of these difficult feelings.

Pictures of a deceased parent and the life they shared can be a wonderful means for the child to maintain a relationship with the parent. Some adult children create an entire wall of pictures that serves as a backdrop for their present life. Some capture a sense of their parent's presence by placing a picture in an area that they see every day. In staying connected they feel strengthened. One of my stepdaughters displays pictures of her mother as well as pictures of her family before her mother died. She makes a point of telling her young children about her mother, their grandmother. It is marvelous that she is giving this new generation a sense of their history. A stepmother can encourage her stepchildren to display pictures of their parent who has died, and if the children are young, she can assist them in doing so. Children of divorce should also be encouraged to display pictures of their absent parent. They, too, may need help to stay connected.

Objects, too, can help the children memorialize and stay connected with the lost parent. My husband gave his daughters their mother's watch and rings, which they wear. Items such as these can be a dear reminder. On my charm bracelet I have a gold emblem of scholastic achievement that was awarded to my mother. It reminds me that she was intelligent and inspires me to think of myself as perhaps inheriting some of her brilliance. Dishes and other domestic items can be displayed and serve as a reminder. My brother always treasured my father's toolbox. He loved to speak of how fine the tools were and claim that he, too, was a good mechanic, "just like Daddy."

Written material of any kind, especially letters, can serve as a powerful connection to the parent who has died. I have a series of letters my mother wrote to my father when I was a toddler. In them she speaks of her love for my father and tells him how cute I am. Needless to say, they are precious!

One of my stepsons who was a hockey star memorialized his mother in a very special way; he honored and remembered her by writing "Mom" on his hockey stick. His mother had loved going to his hockey games and often bragged about how well he played. Hockey was a joy they shared. He continued to feel her presence by having her name on his stick.

Special places, too, can be meaningful and help our stepchildren to stay connected. Visiting the cemetery might appeal to some children as a way to feel close to their dead parent. I don't know how often my stepchildren visited their mother's grave, but I do remember one of the children placing a lily on her grave at Easter. I wish I had been aware enough to realize how comforting these visits to her burial site may have been for them. I wish I had spoken to them about it, wish I had presented it as a way of staying connected to their mother. Interestingly, I visited her grave frequently, as I often took my daily walks in the cemetery. If I were concerned about one of her children, I would tell her all about it and ask her to help me. I never knew her, but I wanted to be connected with her. I am sure her children must have felt an enormous need to be close to her.

Even something as simple as a favorite flower, song, or color can bring us into our parent's presence. One of my friends painted the walls of a small room in her house purple, her mother's favorite color. She says that when she sits quietly in that room she feels embraced by her mother. My mother's favorite music was Chopin; she played it for endless hours. Every time I hear Chopin, I hear my mother play.

"One who is not forgotten is not dead." This poetic expression calls us as stepmothers to encourage and assist our stepchildren to remember and memorialize their parent who has died. This is not as easy as it sounds. We, as stepmothers, have our own insecurities to deal with. Pictures and objects of a dead spouse or dead parent can be threatening; hearing about the idealized deceased person can be intimidating and discouraging. In the early years I was too insecure to encourage my stepchildren to display pictures of their mother or to talk about her, nor was I aware of how helpful it could have been for them.

Becoming a stepmother of five children at the age of thirty-three was difficult and triggered many insecurities within me. When I look back at those first years I see times when I was numbed by it all, simply overwhelmed with the external tasks of laundry, cleaning, and cooking; I was not always able to see and be sensitive to the inner needs and grieving of my stepchildren. Although I sincerely wish I had been more aware and attentive, I do not feel burdened with guilt about what I did not do. I did what I knew and what I could. Stepmothering is a complex task; each of us brings unique gifts as well as certain insecurities and inadequacies. We need to be gentle in judging our failures. Years ago my brother gave me a plaque that read, "Be patient with me, I'm not done yet." That is an excellent maxim for stepmothers!

Healing After the Death of a Spouse

Some stepmothers enter the stepfamily as widows, having lost their former partner to death. The trauma of the death of a spouse creates intense anguish and pain. I have not experienced the death of a spouse, but it seems to me that the sense of powerlessness would be incredible. At least in a divorce someone made a decision; there was a measure of choice. Death, however, happens completely out of our control. It is thrust upon us, often without warning or preparation.

The amount of unresolved grief that a widowed woman brings to the stepfamily is dependent in great part on the amount of time she has had to process her grief before entering a new marriage. Her recovery, like that of her divorced counterpart, is complex and ongoing. She, too, must search out every resource possible to heal herself. Her faith in God, her family, her friends, and the health community are essential components of her recovery. Grief can be a persistent visitor, never sensing when it has worn out its welcome. It cannot, however, be denied its due. Avoidance of grief leads to confusion and depression. One of my friends who has recently been widowed speaks of her grief as being demanding; it comes when she least expects it and stays as long it wants. It is unyielding, exhausting, and demands her utmost integrity; it insists that she grieve honestly. Grief may be a harsh taskmaster, but its rewards of truth and transformation merit our attention.

The husband/father in the stepfamily may also have suffered the loss of a dream through divorce or death. He, too, may bring a portion of grief to the stepfamily. It may, however, be more diffi- cult to recognize his grief, because men grieve very differently than women. Grief is not gender determined, and the grief a man experi- ences, though often not as visible, equals the grief of a woman. The expression may be different, but the intensity is not.

Most women approach their grief with tears and verbalization; they are emotionally orientated, cry easily, and tell their story and feelings over and over to whomever will listen. Most men, how- ever, are not so readily disposed to speak of their pain or shed their tears; they keep their emotions private. They tend to think their way through their grief; frequently seeking refuge in work or by pursuing distraction through sports. Unresolved grief in men fre- quently shows itself in behaviors that are difficult for women to understand. This can put an enormous strain on a marriage. The basic differences between men and women that John Gray speaks of in his book *Men Are from Mars, Women Are from Venus*[15] are apparent in how each copes with loss. Whatever the manner, every man and every woman must process his or her own grief.

If the husband in the newly formed stepfamily has lost his former mate to death, it is likely that he may still be grieving her death. This is definitely a disturbing thought for the new wife. How can she deal with her husband's grief over another woman's death? It is not easy, that's for sure! It is important for the woman to rise above feeling personally threatened and to remember that this man she has fallen in love with is a composite of all that has happened in his life. Everything she loves about him has been shaped by those events and circumstances. If it is true that he is still grieving, it does not mean that he loves her any less. His grief is not a reflection on her; it is his grief, his anguish, and his journey to make. More than likely he will be unable to share his grief with her, and it probably would not be helpful for her or for their relationship if he did. The most important thing she can do for him and for their relationship is to recognize his grief and to accept where he is in the process of resolving it. The greatest gift she has to offer him is her trust. She needs to have confidence that her unconditional love for him will hasten his healing and energize their married relationship.

Ultimately it is always love that heals a broken heart. It was love that gave birth to the newly formed stepfamily, and it is love that will heal and free them from grief. As the individual members of the stepfamily tentatively reach out to each other, new bonds are created, new strengths discovered. Like the newborn fawn, who on its wobbly legs learns with persistent effort how to stand upright and run with joy, the newborn stepfamily with time, effort, and love will heal and experience the joy of a new beginning.

For Your Personal Growth

Exercises:

1. Select a place that has given you pleasure and peace in the past. Plan to visit that place at regular intervals whether it be every day or three times a week. Give yourself that small gift of serenity without feeling guilt or pressure.[16]

2. Consider reaching out to other women who may be grieving a death or divorce.

3. Creatively seek out ways in which you can help your children and stepchildren stay connected to their absent or deceased parent.

Scripture:

Slowly read and let your heart be consoled by God's call to you in your role as comforter in a family that is grieving:

The spirit of the Lord GOD is upon me,
because the LORD has anointed me;
he has sent me to bring good news to the oppressed,
to bind up the brokenhearted,
to proclaim liberty to the captives,
and release to the prisoners;
to provide for those who mourn in Zion—
to give them a garland instead of ashes,
the oil of gladness instead of mourning,
the mantle of praise instead of a faint spirit.
They will be called oaks of righteousness,
the planting of the LORD, to display his glory.
They shall build up the ancient ruins,
they shall raise up the former devastations;

they shall repair the ruined cities,
the devastations of many generations.
For as the earth brings forth its shoots,
and as a garden causes what is sown in it to spring up,
so the Lord God will cause righteousness and praise
to spring up before all the nations.
(Isaiah 61:1, 3-4, 11)

NOTES

1. J. William Worden, *Children and Grief: When a Parent Dies* (New York: Guilford, 1996), 83.

2. "Divorce Statistics Collection," www.divorcereform.org/stats.html.

3. Judith S. Wallerstein, Julia M. Lewis, and Sandra Blakeslee, *The Unexpected Legacy of Divorce: A 25 Year Landmark Study* (New York: Hyperion, 2000), xix, xxiii, 15.

4. E. Mavis Hetherington and John Kelly, *For Better or for Worse: Divorce Reconsidered* (New York: Norton & Company, 2002), 280.

5. Hetherington and Kelly, 138.

6. Hetherington and Kelly, 127 (paraphrase).

7. Hetherington and Kelly, 10.

8. An annulment is not, as is sometimes thought, a "Catholic divorce." It does not deny the reality of the marriage, nor does it make the children of that marriage illegitimate. It is rather the recognition that there were, initially in the marriage, conditions and issues that were inherent obstacles to the development of a mutually loving and faithful relationship that characterizes a marriage that is a sign and sacrament of the faithful, self-giving, and compassionate love of God.

9. Hetherington and Kelly, 280.

10. Worden, 9.

11. Worden, 147–149.

12. Hope Edelman, *Motherless Daughters: The Legacy of Loss* (New York: Dell Publishing, 1994).

13. Worden, 146.

14. Maxine Harris, *The Loss That Is Forever: The Lifelong Impact of the Early Death of a Mother or Father* (New York: Penguin Books, 1995).

15. John Gray, *Men Are from Mars, Women Are from Venus* (New York: HarperCollins, 1992).

16. Carol Staudacher, *A Time to Grieve: Meditations for Healing After the Death of a Loved One* (New York: HarperCollins, 1994), 172–173.

CHAPTER 5

Do You Take . . . This Dog?

Modern research has documented the incredible capacity animals have to give us emotional comfort, to inspire happiness, and even to physically heal. In his book *The Healing Power of Pets*, Marty Becker talks about this amazing ability of animals. He documents how having a pet lessens stress and can even lower cholesterol. Becker cites research studies indicating that the survival rate of people who have had a heart attack is eight times greater if they have a pet. These studies show that simply by petting a dog, blood pressure and heart rate can be lowered by as much as 50 percent.[1]

Dogs have always been a part of my life, in fact so much so, that when Leonard asked me to marry him, he understood that the proposal included not only my three boys but also Samantha, our family dog.

"Do you take this woman, these boys, and this dog . . . ?" He did, and that was four dogs ago! The first, Samantha, was a hearty, gorgeous, disobedient Siberian husky. It is Samantha whose image is portrayed in our first family picture. True, she had to share the stage with a cat or two, but it was she who was the family mascot, she who was our companion, our comforter, and our joy.

Eisenhower, whom we called Ike, was the second four-legged companion of our blended family. He was a German shepherd, fabulously attractive and brilliant. Maggie was third in line. She was a lovely, very blond golden retriever whose one aim in life was to love and be loved. She had no repertoire of tricks and performed no tasks; she didn't fetch, rarely barked, and would probably dis-integrate on the spot if someone were to raise a hand against me. She was astutely aware of my every mood and emotion and was quick to comfort me, to join me in joy, or to be silently with me in solitude. We all loved her dearly.

Emily is the dog of the moment and is probably the "dog of my life." An incredibly lovely silver standard poodle, she is wonder-fully affectionate, playful, and sweet—a constant source of joy and comfort! We are deeply touched by her spirit and regard her as a special revelation of God's goodness.

All of nature is a revelation of God. All creatures uniquely reflect the spirit of God. When we are deeply bonded with an animal, we become aware that "the things that make life most precious and blessed—courage and daring, conscience and compassion, imagi-nation and originality, fantasy and play—do not belong to our kind alone."[2] All of life has a share in the indwelling creative splendor of God. Animals may not have human form; the degree of conscious-ness of animals may differ; but in some marvelous and inexpress-ible way, God's presence is reflected in them. Those of us who are in a loving, truly mutual relationship with an animal experience the touch of the divine in the faithful and unconditional love they extend to us.

Samantha deserves a special acknowledgement. I got her for my sons and myself at the time of my divorce. I remembered how my dogs comforted me as a child, and I thought that having a dog might help us deal with the trauma of the divorce.

It was a crisp spring day when the four of us drove to the coun-try to visit the farm where Siberian huskies were bred. It seemed like there were thousands of huskies all barking at the same time. I had a moment of alarm: "What was I getting myself into?" All hesitation evaporated when we saw the puppies! What a difficult task it was to make a choice. It was not long, however, until one beguiling little female won our hearts. The boys named her Samantha after the woman in the television series *Bewitched*. From that time on she cast her sweet spell upon all of us!

Samantha's family grew when I remarried, and with the family's growth she blossomed. In fact, she really blossomed! Shortly after our marriage, Leonard and the children were sledding down the hill in our backyard, when Leonard noticed Samantha, who was ordinarily very robust, struggling to get up the hill. A few days later she gave birth to five little puppies. It was just what our new family needed. The puppies were wonderful! We had just come together as a family; new hope had been born; but there was also a great deal of fear, confusion, disruption, and, I am sure, some anger. The puppies provided a delightful diversion and helped to defuse the emotionally laden environment of our family. We all gathered around the puppies, awestruck and cooing.

Samantha was a member of our family. Her presence was therapeutic; she provided a safe zone. She was always there, always willing to listen, to play, to comfort.

Dogs are remarkably aware, since their perception is unclouded by reason and cognizant distractions. "They are able to sense what is going on. They can smell it, and they can feel it."[3] Psychiatrists and psychologists prescribe pets for emotional problems, such as post-traumatic stress, social anxiety disorder, or depression. Dogs have provided assistance to people who are blind for years, and dogs and even monkeys have been a great help to people confined to wheelchairs. Now there are specially trained dogs for the hearing impaired as well as dogs that are trained to alert their guardians to the onset of seizures or to alert people suffering from bipolar disease to the onset of a manic state.

What some dogs are capable of doing for people with whom they are deeply bonded is truly impressive. Samantha was not trained for anything. In fact, I don't think she was particularly intelligent. But she loved us, she simply loved us; and her love helped us. Just being around her seemed to miraculously defuse negativity: anger subsided, calmness was restored, and spontaneous play and laughter emerged. Children who have suffered the loss of a parent through death or the loss of their family of origin through divorce are emotionally burdened and can become overly serious. A pet can serve to draw them out of their shells and help them to become playful.

Samantha also played a significant role in my adjustment as a stepmother. In the summer she accompanied me on my daily walks down the lake road, and in the winter she was my companion on my long walks through the city cemetery. I remember one Sunday evening a couple weeks after we were married. I was in the laundry room, feeling overwhelmed. I looked longingly into the adjoining family room where the rest of the family was watching television. I am sure I could have joined them, but at the time I felt stressed and sorry for myself. Suddenly the ironing caddy that was overloaded with heavy wet corduroys fell. It was the last straw! I burst into tears, put on my heavy sheepskin coat, and ran out into the cold winter night, taking Samantha with me. We walked and walked, and I told her all about it: "Maybe I made a mistake. Perhaps I am not able to handle this large family. Perhaps I do not have what it takes to love another woman's children." We walked for hours. Finally we stopped to rest under a large pine tree, where I cried all my tears into her soft, fluffy winter coat. When at last we returned home, I felt relieved and calm and had miraculously made plans of ways that I could lighten the laundry load.

I am not suggesting that every stepfamily needs a pet to survive. There are some people for whom it would not work or circumstances that would not make it possible. Marvelous as they are, pets can be very frustrating. Acquiring a pet is not to be taken lightly. It is, after all, a responsibility that requires a substantial expenditure of energy, time, and resources. Pets must be trained, exercised, and groomed; there are food bills and veterinarian bills as well as the unexpected expense—accidental, for sure—of nearly ruined furniture or carpeting.

The choice of a pet is important. When making a selection, you need to consider such factors as the children's allergies, their comfort level around animals, and their ability help care for the animal. Other factors to consider are the amount of space in your yard and the effect that the animal will have on your house. Dogs make excellent companions, but they need someone to walk them as well as room to run and play. Cats are easier to care for, but they don't bond to people as readily as dogs do. Birds are often very entertaining, particularly those who can mimic speech. (My sister had a bird that called her to get up in the morning.) Yet birds can get lonely and develop emotional problems if they don't get enough attention, so they aren't always the best pets for children. Rabbits are fun to watch and hold, but they chew furniture and electrical cords when they live in the house. In *The Healing Power of Pets*, Becker suggests that families consider these and other issues when searching for a pet.[4] Having a pet does not work for all families; it is imperative to look at the disadvantages as well as the advantages to discern if it is right for your family. I am grateful that it worked for ours.

Our pets gave us the grace of their loving animal presence. I continue to marvel at my dog's faithfulness and her sensitivity of response. Emily and I are enjoying each other immensely. The ritual of our daily walks and the quiet togetherness contribute to the well-being of each of us. We love being together, lovingly present to each other.

For Your Personal Growth

Questions for reflection:

1. Indulge yourself with the memory of a favorite childhood pet. What did you love about it? Was it comforting?

2. If you do not have a pet, would you like one? Would your family benefit from having a pet?

NOTES

1. Marty Becker with Danelle Morton, *The Healing Power of Pets: Harnessing the Amazing Ability of Pets to Make and Keep People Happy and Healthy* (New York: Hyperion, 2002), 73.

2. Gary Kowalski, *The Souls of Animals* (Walpole, N.H.: Stillpoint Publishing, 1991), 111.

3. Becker, 144.

4. Becker, 188.

CHAPTER 6

"You're Not My Mother!"

Sometimes stepmothers try to win the love of their stepchildren too quickly. A beautiful Ethiopian fairy tale illustrates this experience.

Once upon a time in the mountains of Ethiopia, there lived a lonely woman well beyond her childbearing years. Her name was Fanaye. She had never been married and lived alone. As the years went by, her feelings of worthlessness and sadness increased. She had so much love in her heart, but there was no one to give it to. She felt as if her life was being wasted.

One day while visiting a neighboring village, Fanaye met a kind man whose name was Tesfa. Tesfa's wife had died, and he, too, was very lonely. They liked each other immediately, and in a short time they were married. Tesfa took his new bride home. He was excited; he had a surprise for Fanaye. The surprise was his son, Abebe. Fanaye was delighted! At last she had a child. She had a son! Abebe, however, was not so thrilled! "You're not my real mother!" he shrieked.

Fanaye was discouraged. She did everything possible to win his affection. She cooked his favorite stews; she mended his clothes. She showered him with the love that, for years, had been stored up in her heart.

"You're not my mother!" he persisted. He wouldn't eat the stew, and after she mended his clothes, he deliberately tore them. Fanaye could do nothing to please him. The harder she tried, the more belligerent he became.

Fanaye became depressed. In desperation, she sought out the wisdom of the village medicine man. She asked him to give her a magic potion that would make Abebe accept and love her. Instead of giving her a potion, the medicine man told her that she must bring him three whiskers from the chin of the fierce old lion that lived near the black rock. She was horrified! How could she possibly approach the ferocious lion?

Several days went by. Finally, she summoned up her courage and made her way to the lion's den. As she drew near she began to tremble with fear and hid herself behind the black rock. After a few minutes she cautiously peeked out from the rock to see if the lion was home. Instantly, he caught sight of her; he had known she was there. Lions do not like intruders; he snarled and growled! Fanaye was terrified and ran away.

The next day she returned, but this time she carried a bundle containing fresh meat. She left the meat some distance from the black rock. When she was safely away, she looked back and saw the lion eating the meat. For several months Fanaye returned to the black rock and left meat. Each day she moved closer and closer to the lion. Finally the day came when the lion took the meat directly from Fanaye's hands. Here was her chance. She stood very still and slowly reached over and plucked three hairs from his chin. The lion did not mind at all. He had grown to trust Fanaye.

Fanaye was overjoyed! She ran to the medicine man. With the three whiskers, he would be able to make the magic potion. Abebe would love her. With triumph she presented the lion's whiskers to the medicine man. Without a moment's hesitation, the medicine man threw the whiskers into the air. Fanaye watched in horror as the precious whiskers disappeared into the wind. She was devastated; all the months of work, all the agony and fear were in vain.

The medicine man looked at Fanaye, his eyes full of compassion. He said to her, "You need no magic charms. You have learned what you need to know. You must approach your stepson as you did the lion, and in this way you will win his love."

Fanaye did what the medicine man told her. She bided her time; she kept her distance. She was to Abebe as she had been to the lion. Over time Abebe saw her gentle goodness. Abebe slowly began to love Fanaye.[1] I suspect that most stepmothers could say, "Been there, done that!"

Even though I was overjoyed with my sons, I had always secretly longed for a daughter. How fortunate I was that my marriage to Leonard gave me three! The youngest was eleven, and I felt instantly drawn to her; she was young enough to be my own child. When her twelfth birthday arrived three weeks after our marriage, I baked her an elaborate "princess" cake and made a princess crown for her head. I wanted her first birthday with me to be special. She loved it! During the weeks that followed, I continued to shower her with attention and affection. At first she responded positively, but slowly she began to withdraw from me; she became pouty and hostile. One morning while she was getting ready for school, I corrected her about some small thing, and she burst out, "You're not my real mother! Leave me alone!"

I knew instantly what I had done. I had overdone! She was a young child who had very recently suffered the tremendous loss of her mother. Here I was, too anxious to claim her as my own, too eager to love her and make her happy.

When I married and received my stepchildren, I was eager to win their love. They were part of the package; it was absolutely essential that we all love each other and, of course, the sooner, the better. There were many times, such as in the case of my youngest stepdaughter, that I was insensitive, moved too fast, or expected too much. The children needed time to adjust, to find their way in this new family. They were, I am sure, still grieving for their mother. They may have perceived my overeagerness as a threat.

Retrospectively I realize that I also felt threatened. I had recently gone through the excruciating pain of a divorce and wanted desperately for my marriage to succeed. In my anxiousness I responded like Fanaye; I was overzealous.

Anxiety was not the only motivation for my overzealous approach with my stepchildren. Since I had three beautiful sons of my own, my heart was not lonely like Fanaye's was. It was, however, filled with sincere compassion for my stepchildren. Their mother had died. She had been only forty-seven; the children were young and vulnerable. Their ages ranged from eleven to eighteen. My own mother had died two years prior to my marriage; she was fifty-three, and I was thirty. I was devastated, and I was an adult. I could only imagine my stepchildren's confusion, hurt, and anger at losing their young, vibrant mother.

Well here I was, ready to love them, ready to make their favorite stews, mend their clothes—whatever it took!

Many times they would not eat the food I made; many times they rejected my efforts at loving them. More than once I heard, "You're not my real mother!" They wanted their own mother. Of course, they wanted their own mother!

Authors James Bray and John Kelly state that some stepparents make the mistake of thinking that just because they want an instant family, they will instantly get one. They emphasize that it takes time and effort to bond with a stepchild and that moving too quickly can be seriously counterproductive.[2]

Each of us, as stepmothers, has our own particular story. Each of us has our own fears, needs, and motivations out of which we respond. All we can do is to do what we can with what we have. The experiences we have had, the wisdom we have gained, as well as the limitations, woundedness, and developmental gaps we ourselves may be burdened with are what we have to work with. We all deeply desire to be loving stepmothers to the children entrusted to us. Much of our married happiness depends on our success, and I believe that most of us try to go too far too fast. I am sure that all of us can identify, in some way and to some degree, with Fanaye's overzealous approach.

And having tried it, we know it does not work!

May this fable of Fanaye show us the slow and patient approach that will open our stepchildren's hearts so that they eventually will come to trust us.

For Your Personal Growth

Questions for reflection:
1. Can you identify with Fanaye's story? If so, in what ways?

2. Do you truly want to love your stepchildren? If so, what motivates you?

ou, at times, perceive your stepchildren resisting your efforts to love them? What would be your wisest response to their resistance?

4. Respect from your stepchildren is nonnegotiable. Can you be content with that while, at the same time, hoping for a loving relationship sometime in the future?

Scripture:

We need not be surprised that healing and the growth of love take time. Let the words of St. Paul be a consolation and encouragement:

Rejoice in hope, be patient in suffering, persevere in prayer. (Romans 12:12)

May the God of steadfastness and encouragement grant you to live in harmony with one another, in accordance with Christ Jesus, so that together you may with one voice glorify the God and Father of our Lord Jesus Christ. (Romans 15:5-6)

NOTES

1. Retold from Nancy Raines Day, *The Lion's Whiskers: An Ethiopian Folktale* (New York: Scholastic, 1995).

2. James Bray and John Kelly, *Stepfamilies: Love, Marriage, and Parenting in the First Decade* (New York: Broadway Books, 1998), 81.

CHAPTER 7

Taking Life Gently through Prayer

As every parent knows, taking care of a family is a demanding job. Being a stepmother in the complexity of a combined family is even more exacting. Living in a gentle, mindful manner seems, most of the time, to be totally out of reach for the stepmother who is bombarded with the numerous emotional needs and expectations that are characteristic of a stepfamily.

There is so much to do: the laundry, the shopping, the cooking, the cleaning. Many if not most stepmothers also work outside the home. True, the husband and children can be enlisted to help, but the organization and brunt of domestic duties tends to fall to the woman—the mother or the stepmother. We can easily feel overwhelmed. Then there are the more important tasks of parenting. In cooperation with our husbands, we set rules, impose limits, settle disputes, and correct behavior.

Managing a combined household and parenting children and stepchildren often require firmness and strength. Yet none of us wants to slip into manipulation and control or to place unreasonable demands on our family. So how can we, as stepmothers, take life gently, and what does it mean to be gentle? How can we nurture gentleness within ourselves so that we will not succumb to forcefulness? How are we to be gentle and yet courageously firm? How can we manage everything?

Nurturing an Attitude of Gentleness through Prayer

Throughout my years of parenting, of being a mother and step-mother, my awareness of the need to nurture within myself an atti-tude of gentleness has consistently been affirmed. It is a simple les-son. Nothing else works!

The need was, first of all, to be gentle toward myself. When I began to aggressively strive for perfection, to ambitiously strain to accomplish more than was comfortably possible, my world would begin to disintegrate. I would become a victim of time urgency, scurrying from one thing to another, pressured by my own unre-alistic expectations. Overextension has been a tendency for me throughout most of my adult life. It has, I know, stemmed from a need for approval and praise. I think many women struggle with this issue. It is as if women have a negative mother hanging over them, always telling them, "You don't measure up; it's not enough; you can do better; you can do more!"

I was forced to look hard at my tendency toward perfection-ism when, at thirty-three, I found myself with eight children, five of them stepchildren, all of them with a measure of neediness. It took only a few weeks for me to realize that I needed to moderate the expectations I placed on myself and on them. I quickly learned my limitations and the counter-productivity of ambitious striving. I realized that if I were to be a loving presence to Leonard and the children, I needed to take good care of myself and to deal with my compulsive behavioral patterns. I had to learn to be gentle with myself, to accept things as they were, to accept life as it happened.

Turning to God for Help

I knew I was unable to discover this way of gentleness by myself. As people do when making the twelve steps in Alcoholics Anony-mous, I committed myself to turning to a power greater than myself.

I turned to God. It was quite natural for me to turn to God in this new need; I had an established pattern of prayer. My early childhood had set the precedent. I had learned long ago that if I opened my heart to God, the way would be shown to me, and the strength for whatever I needed would be given. Each of us deals with life in our own way. I intuitively knew that, for me, the only way was to cultivate an attitude of gentleness through an intimate relationship with God.

I drew on my religious background. My mother's family was Catholic, and my father's family was grounded in a Scripture-oriented, Quaker-like tradition. My mother, although prayerful, never read the Bible. I never saw my father read it either, but my paternal grandparents read it daily. As a little girl, I would sit on Grandpa's knee while he read Bible stories to me. At that young age, I was far more interested in the sugarcoated orange slice that was my reward for sitting quietly than I was in the stories. I could never have imagined then what a gift those quiet times would come to be for me.

At the time of my divorce, when my life unraveled, the image of my grandparents praying with their Bible was the inspiration for me to turn to Scripture for direction and comfort. My use of Scripture grew through the years. Faced with the complexities of our stepfamily and the heightened realization of my dependency on God, prayer became a priority of my daily life, with Scripture its primary focus.

Feeling that prayer was absolutely essential, I was faithful to my commitment. It was, however, somewhat of a struggle. I did not have any guidance in how to use the Scriptures. I followed the readings for the seasons of the church year, and although I enjoyed them, I felt removed from them—as if I were on the outside looking ιot become discouraged, though; I persisted, and my effort was sincere. My need was great, and I was not about to give up. I decided, however, that I needed a mentor.

I had gotten into the habit of resting an hour before the children arrived home from school, a recouping time after the tasks of the day and before meeting the onslaught of after-school activities. Unless I was completely exhausted, I would read during that time. One afternoon I picked up an obscure booklet that someone had given me. In it I read about the Spiritual Exercises of St. Ignatius.[1] This was just what I needed! I was excited at the discovery of such exercises, exhilarated about their potential. The booklet explained how the exercises represented a specific pattern for prayer, a pattern that used Scripture and followed the life of Christ. I was not deterred by the fact that these Christ-centered exercises of conversion were developed in the sixteenth century by a saint named Ignatius; even though centuries separated us, I instinctively knew that the exercises were right for me.

Going away to a retreat house for a month of prayer is the customary way to make the exercises. There is, however, a way of making them at home during the course of daily life. This approach, known as the Nineteenth Annotation, usually takes about a year. Since I couldn't possibly go away for a month, the Nineteenth Annotation was perfect for me. I set out to find someone who could help me begin my journey. It was not long until someone trained in the spirituality of the exercises and in Ignatian spirituality surfaced. She was willing to be my spiritual director.

Approaching Scripture as a Love Letter

The first thing she taught me was to approach Scripture like a love letter, reading each passage over and over, savoring its delights, absorbing the energy of love.

I knew about love letters and how deeply they can touch us.

My father and mother had died in 1967, fifty-three days apart. My mother died of cancer, and my father of an accident. They had had a tumultuous marriage and were, in many ways, mismatched. I always wondered why they married and if they loved each other. The circumstances of their marriage prompted me to question whether they had really wanted me or whether I had been nothing more than an accident.

One day as I was writing at my desk, I looked closely at the configuration of my handwriting and wondered if it resembled my mother's, whose script I remembered as being very beautiful. I realized that I didn't have a single scrap of her handwriting and thought how precious it would be to have one. Three days later I received a phone call from a cousin who lived some distance away and whom I rarely saw. She said she wanted to see me and that she had a surprise for me. I knew that she had in her possession an extraordinary vase that had belonged to my grandmother. She knew how much I loved the vase, and she was also aware of the deep love I had for my grandmother. I was confident that her surprise for me would be the vase. We planned to meet at a halfway mark so that the trip would be shorter for both of us.

When the day of the meeting arrived, I was excited. I had mentally placed the coveted vase in a favorite spot and was eager to claim it. But the moment I saw the shape of the package my cousin held, I knew it couldn't be the vase. When I saw her eyes begin to fill with tears, I knew that her gift must be far more important. It was. She handed me a scrapbook that she had come upon while walking in an alley near her home. It had lain on the ground next to an incinerator barrel from which it had apparently fallen. It was my father's scrapbook, and in it were love letters written to him in my mother's hand.

How miraculous was that? When I was two years old, my mother and father had lived apart for a winter so that my father could go off to find work. My mother had written the letters to him while he was away. There were five of them in all. In the letters, Mother spoke of her love for Daddy, how much she missed him, and how darling I was—how lucky they were to have a little girl like me. She closed her letters with, "Must close, Darling. Wish we were together. I love you with all my heart, Agnes and Jacque." I had wished to have just a sample of my mother's handwriting. Instead, I had gotten love letters! I read and reread them. Like a thirsty sponge, I soaked up the words of love, allowing them to sink into the depths of me and heal me. I know about love letters. I know their healing power.

The love letter approach to Scripture, which is at the core of Ignatian meditation, invites us to allow God's all-embracing and healing love to be absorbed deep within our hearts. It enables us to surrender our fears: "Do not fear, for I am with you" (Isaiah 43:5). I had many fears during the years when the children were growing up. When their pain erupted in destructive behavior, I experienced intense anxiety and confusion; I did not know the best course of action to help them, and I was afraid for them. I was afraid for myself and for our marriage. Could I sustain my love and faithfulness throughout all that was happening? Would our marriage survive? Reading Scripture as a love letter from God comforted and reassured me.

I particularly recall one day when I was nearly overwhelmed with worry about my youngest son. I was in church and read the Gospel of St. John where it says, "Go; your son will live" (John 4:50). I took those words into my heart; I believed them. They transformed my anxiety into confidence. My son was healed! It didn't happen overnight, but almost immediately I felt the energy shift within him.

Over the years, the words of John 4:50 have continued to instill in my heart a confident reassurance of his well-being—that God will be with him, care for him, and protect him—and they continue to impart comfort and peace. The regular discipline of praying with Scripture daily using the love letter approach was deeply healing and supportive.

Learning to Pray with Our Senses

The next step in using Scripture to pray involves contemplating those passages where there is some action, such as when the angel appears to Mary, Jesus is born, or Jesus turns water into wine. There are many rich and revealing stories in the Bible. To read them is one thing; to allow oneself to be drawn into them is quite another. In the Ignatian tradition this process is called contemplation. My spiritual director proceeded to teach me this new kind of prayer.

She taught me that St. Ignatius trained his followers to be attentive to their senses. It is through our five senses—touch, taste, hearing, sight, and smell—that the Spirit reveals God's presence. Each sense nurtures our spiritual growth and calls us into a personal relationship with God. We are, after all, human. What better way for God to communicate with us than through our humanness?

My director told me to enter into a Scripture passage with my imagination. What kind of day was it? Was it cold or warm, was the sun blazing, or was it raining? She instructed me to allow myself to enter into the day. What were the sounds? Did I hear the sounds of a crowd, the roar of a mighty wind, or only the gentle whisperings of leaves? Were there smells in the air? Did I detect the musky scent of animals and hay, the aroma of exotic foods cooking, or perhaps the sweet fragrance of flowers in bloom? Was anyone with me? What were they doing, and what were their facial expressions? Where was I in the passage? Was I off to the side, or was I close to the event? Was I participating? What were the textures I was feeling? Were they rough like burlap cloth, hard like rock, or smooth like silk? Was I eating? What were the flavors?

I was immediately enthusiastic about opening myself to Scripture in this manner. I loved using my imagination; I have a theatrical bent that would easily take to this method. I had enjoyed using the love letter approach with the passages that were not action oriented, and this sounded even more wonderful. I couldn't wait to begin.

One of the Scripture passages I was given for my prayer was from Genesis 22, where God told Abraham to go up the mountain and sacrifice his son Isaac as a burnt offering. I struggled when I began to imagine the passage. I had thought it would be easy, but it was not. I became stymied. How did Abraham feel about offering his son as a sacrifice? How did Isaac feel? I had no experience with which to connect. My relationship with my father had been limited. There were only a few instances in which his love for me was concretely evident. Initially the passage only served to remind me of this sadness that I had always carried.

I felt a little panic build within me; this was not going to work. I prayed for help and doggedly continued. Making a great effort, I imagined walking with Abraham and Isaac in the hot sun up the steep mountain, my breath coming in gasps. I watched as Isaac struggled with the bundle of wood he carried on his shoulders. He was only a young boy; the wood was far too heavy for him. I looked at his confused expression, which seemed to say, "What's going on? What is Father doing?"

Suddenly, into my mind came the image of my son, Thomas, who was in the bunkhouse with a severe headache and a slight fever. There had been several cases of encephalitis in the area. What if Thomas had encephalitis? I knew that the possibility was remote, but the mere thought of it was excruciating. Thomas, whom I loved with all my heart! What would I do if something were to happen to him, if he were to die? In an instant, my heart was overflowing with love for him, for all the children. I was flooded with a sense of their absolute preciousness. I now thought I knew, deep within, how Abraham felt. I may not have been able to connect as a child with my father, but I was able to connect as a mother with my son. I knew Abraham's anguish. And in a sudden burst of awareness, I felt God's love for me. It was like my love for Thomas, like Abraham's love for Isaac. God cared for me. God is my father, my mother, who doesn't want to see me hurt or in pain.

What an amazing revelation this prayer came to be. Working through my imagination, the Holy Spirit moved beyond the gap of my experience of fatherlessness and brought me into the embrace of God's love. This single prayer experience has empowered me throughout all these years. A new receptivity was born within me that day: My heart was opened in trust—trust to receive and give love.

That was just one experience of praying with all of my senses. There were so many more ahead of me. Not all passages and prayer experiences have been as revealing to me as that first one. Many were, however, and many continue to be. I grew in the belief that God would always be present when I opened myself in prayer, when I was receptive to a personal relationship with him. I knew it was unrealistic to always expect "flash-of-lightning" experiences. There were many days, especially if I had allowed myself to get overtired, when my experience of prayer was frustrating, horribly distracted, or intolerably dry. On those days praying seemed like an utter waste of time, but gradually my experience revealed to me that my sense of God's presence wasn't dependent upon feelings. I didn't have to feel God's presence in order for God to be there. I came to realize that what was important was to show up and make what effort I could. I became more aware that God's power, even when it takes the form of a small seed, will always be watered and nourished to grow by a sincere effort at prayer. And how sorely I was in need of that power! The children served as a constant reminder of that!

These two basic forms of praying with Scripture have proven to be a godsend to me. Although I never became the perfect mother or stepmother, prayer has made an incredible difference in my life. It continually moves me forward on my lifelong task of growing in gentleness both toward myself and others, and of healing and transformation. Praying with Scripture, in the manner of the sixteenth-century saint Ignatius, has enabled me to be a better woman, a more loving wife to my husband, and certainly a much better stepmother and mother. I may have survived without it, but I cannot imagine the tatters I would have left in my path.

My efforts to care for myself through prayer were transformed into the gentle and tender care of God on my behalf, revealed through his word in Scripture. It is through God's word that we, as stepmothers, will receive the Spirit's gift of gentleness.

Loving and compassionate God, open our hearts to receive the gift of your transforming word.

For Your Personal Growth

Question for reflection:

Is there something in your family's spiritual tradition that offers you a potential for strength and encouragement? If so, would it be worth nurturing a discipline of that spirituality? Is there a spiritual discipline to which you feel drawn?

Scripture:

1. Prayerfully read Isaiah 43:1-5. Think of it as a love letter from God written to you. In the place of "Israel" and "Jacob" substitute your own name:

> *But now thus says the* LORD,
>   *he who created you, O Jacob,*
>   *he who formed you, O Israel:*
> *Do not fear, for I have redeemed you;*
>   *I have called you by name, you are mine.*
> *When you pass through the waters, I will be with you;*
>   *and through the rivers, they shall not overwhelm you;*
> *when you walk through fire you shall not be burned,*
>   *and the flame shall not consume you.*
> *For I am the* LORD *your God,*
>   *the Holy One of Israel, your Savior. . . .*
> *[Y]ou are precious in my sight,*
>   *and honored, and I love you. . . .*
> *Do not fear, for I am with you.*

2. Read Mark 10:46-52. Imagine yourself as the blind person. What kind of day was it? Who was present with you? Jesus asks, "What do you want me to do for you?" How do you answer him?

They came to Jericho. As he and his disciples and a large crowd were leaving Jericho, Bartimaeus son of Timaeus, a blind beggar, was sitting by the roadside. When he heard that it was Jesus of Nazareth, he began to shout out and say, "Jesus, Son of David, have mercy on me!" Many sternly ordered him to be quiet, but he cried out even more loudly, "Son of David, have mercy on me!" Jesus stood still and said, "Call him here." And they called the blind man, saying to him, "Take heart; get up, he is calling you." So throwing off his cloak, he sprang up and came to Jesus. Then Jesus said to him, "What do you want me to do for you?" The blind man said to him, "My teacher, let me see again." Jesus said to him, "Go; your faith has made you well." Immediately he regained his sight and followed him on the way.

NOTES

1. It has only been in the last thirty years or so, since Vatican II, that the Exercises of St. Ignatius have been made more available to lay people. The exercises and the Examen of Consciousness (see Chapter 8, "Moving Away from Negativity," for a detailed discussion of the examen) have always formed the basis of the spirituality of the Society of Jesus (Jesuits), the followers of Ignatius. While used primarily in religious congregations for centuries, they were originally intended for the common people The mandates of Vatican II required that religious congregations reflect back to the original charism of their founders and reappropriate their teaching for the modern church. Since that time, the Jesuit congregation and others founded on Ignatian spirituality have made great strides in imparting Ignatian spirituality to the laity. From my experience and perspective, the availability of the Exercises of St. Ignatius and the Examen of Consciousness is among the greatest gifts to have come out of Vatican II.

A contemporary manual for directing a retreat using the Spiritual Exercises can be found in David L. Fleming, *A Contemporary Reading of the Spiritual Exercises: A Companion to St. Ignatius' Text*

(St. Louis: Institute of Jesuit Sources, 1976). In the *Take and Receive* series by Jacqueline Syrup Bergan and Marie Schwan, the *Spiritual Exercises* are made available in five volumes (*Love*, *Forgiveness*, *Birth*, *Surrender*, and *Freedom*) as a self-help guide to prayer. For these volumes, as well as *Praying with Ignatius of Loyola*, also by Bergan and Schwan, see the bibliography.

CHAPTER 8

Moving Away from Negativity

A new stepfamily can be a minefield of intense, explosive emotions. The last thing we want to do is add to this minefield with our own catalog of negative and critical attitudes. When I married my husband, I felt privileged to receive my five stepchildren and humbled to be entrusted with loving and caring for them. Yet, when stressed with the conflicts of mothering this family, I found that I could easily slip into a "victim" stance. Before I even realized it, something would trigger the reaction, and the tape of negativity would begin to roll: "I have so much to do. No one sees what I do. No one appreciates anything! If I complain, they'll just think I'm the wicked stepmother."

Negativity can be an incredibly destructive force. In her insightful book *Anatomy of the Spirit: The Seven Stages of Power and Healing*, Caroline Myss relates that when we harbor negative emotions toward others or toward ourselves, we poison ourselves physically and spiritually. She believes that negativity can actually make us ill—that our "biography becomes our biology"![1]

Unfortunately, I had trouble recognizing the signs of my own negativity early enough to stop it; one small issue could easily snowball into something ugly. I wanted to be positive and to be aware of God's presence in the ordinary activities of my daily life. Thankfully, I found a time-honored process to heighten my awareness so that I could put on the brakes at the first inclination toward negativity and become more keenly aware of God's presence. It is a discernment process called the Examen of Consciousness, and is usually taught in conjunction with the *Spiritual Exercises of St. Ignatius.*

Rooted in the incarnation, Christians have always been drawn to see God in all things and all things in God. Many holy people of history have given us various methods of reflecting on and discerning circumstances and events in our lives to determine whether they are of the good or of the evil spirit. One of the most enduring of these is the Examen of Consciousness given to us by St. Ignatius.

In the beginning, I thought that the title, Examen of Consciousness, sounded rather presumptuous and that the talk of good and evil spirits seemed archaic. Our contemporary world is shy of thinking and speaking of the sacred, much less contemplating and conversing about spirit, good or otherwise. Our art, literature, theater, and films are replete with themes of good and evil, but collectively our everyday orientation does not venture in that direction. However, despite my doubts, I was eager to learn. I sensed the great potential of this prayer practice.

A Simple, Daily Practice

The examen is a simple prayer practice in which we discover how God has been present to us and how we have responded to that presence during the day. It is not to be confused with an examination of conscience, in which we are concerned about how we have failed. It is, rather, an exploration of how God has been present within the events, circumstances, and feelings of our daily lives.

This examen takes only ten or fifteen minutes. I have always done it in the evening, but some people find it helpful to do it midday or at the end of their work day. I like to write my daily examen in a journal. Writing my reflections seems to help me clarify my thoughts; moreover I appreciate looking back through my journal to see how my contemplation has been evolving, how God has been transforming my life.

Marian Cowan and John Futrell, noted authors of works on Ignatian spirituality, observe that there are five steps to the examen that reflect the dynamic movement of personal love—that is, the words we want to say to our beloved and the order in which we want to say them: Thank you . . . Help me . . . I love you . . . I'm sorry . . . Be with me.[2]

In the first step, "thank you," we declare our dependency on God and give thanks for the gifts of the day. These gifts are the ordinary things of life. In reflecting on them we realize God's presence within them. The list could include the warmth of the sun on your face, a baby's little foot peeking out from a blanket, or the laughter of your husband. The smallest moment can serve to heighten our awareness of how unconditionally God loves us. We need only to reflectively open ourselves to see the wonderment of life.

The second step, "help me," is a prayer of love in which we acknowledge our belief that God works through and in our lives to reveal our true selves to us. We pray for an increased awareness of how God is guiding and shaping our lives. We pray also for a more sensitive awareness of the obstacles we put in God's way.

We ask for what we want. We pray for guidance in the second step because we need God's help to distinguish the subtle differences between good and evil. This prayer leads us into the third step.

In the third step, "I love you," we reflect on God's loving presence in the events of the day and in the feelings we experienced during that day. We look back on the events of the day and how we responded. For example, at some time during the day I may have encountered a difficult conflict with a child. How did I feel? Did anger begin to well up in my stomach? Did I feel overwhelmed and discouraged? Were these feelings the movement of evil or of good? What does God call me to when I experience a conflict with a child? Or, perhaps I was in a group of women, and the conversation deteriorated into gossip. What did that feel like? If we are astute, we will be sensitive to what it feels like when things are moving in a negative direction. In other words, we will be sensitive to the movement of evil. What is God's call in such a situation?

The task during this step of the examen is to discern where, during the day, we have experienced the movement of the good spirit within us and where we have experienced the movement of the evil spirit influencing us. The movement of the good spirit is referred to in Ignatian spirituality as *consolation,* and the movement of the evil spirit as *desolation.* I have always appreciated that terminology because negativity, with its accompanying feelings, is uncomfortable and discomforting, while the movements of the good spirit, such as gentleness, kindness, or appropriate expressions of anger, are consoling and comforting.

Again, it is not always easy to tell if the movement is of the good or evil spirit. For example, if we are unjustly treated, anger is the appropriate response. Anger, in itself, is not necessarily of the evil spirit. The call is to express and deal with it in a noncombative and productive manner—to respond, not to react. Sometimes the evil spirit may come disguised as an "angel of light." An example would be if I, as a stepmother, were to conceive of doing something extraordinary for one of my stepchildren that, while appearing to look like an exercise in self-sacrifice, is actually motivated by my desire to impress my husband and win his adulation.

The fourth step, "I'm sorry," is a plea for God's loving forgiveness and healing. There may be many situations that happened during the day that we would like healed and forgiven, but it is most helpful to choose only one specific event. One can say or write, "The event or situation that I most want healed is _____."

The fifth step, "be with me," is a prayer of entrusting oneself to God's loving care. I ask God to share with me whatever gift of the Holy Spirit's presence I most need. For example, if I have been harsh during the day, I ask for a share in the gentleness of God. "Be with me in _____."

The examen is the kind of process one becomes more adept at with regular use. It has been a great help for me. Without my examen, my daily prayerful reflection on the day, I know I would have missed appreciating many sacred moments of my family and my life. I am also aware that my examen saved me from many serious mistakes. Most important, without the examen, my mistakes might not have been occasions for growth. In reflecting on the events and feelings of the day, it is very hard to bask in denial. Eventually, one realizes that there are areas in which growth is necessary or perhaps that apologies are needed.

In one of his sermons, the fourteenth-century German mystic Meister Eckhart spoke of the "spark of the soul." That spark is the heightened experience we have of God's presence and grace in the circumstances and events of our lives. It can help us by clarifying what draws us away from God and what draws us toward our truest nature in God. "The spark of the soul, which is created by God, is a light pressed in from above. It is the image of the divine nature, and it is always turned toward the good."[3] It works against that which is not pure, and it always attracts to the good. Our minds and spirits are in a state of prepared readiness with the daily practice of the examen; through prayerful reflection we anticipate and become fully receptive for the spark of our souls to ignite our hearts.

One of the first times I experienced the grace of the examen was in the early years when I first began praying it. I had been having great difficulty establishing a relationship with my youngest step-daughter. Feelings of anger, rebellion, and distrust were swirling around us. It seemed like both of us would "lose it" at least once every day. For many weeks my examen read, "Please heal my rela-tionship with Stacy." Then one night, when writing down the gifts of the day, I automatically wrote "Stacy." My eyes filled with tears; the relationship had gone from chaos to love. I was given a darling young girl to love. I had, with God's grace, made the journey from victim to privileged. Now she is a mature, beautiful young woman. I am grateful beyond measure for her presence in my life.

Examen of Consciousness

Thank you:
God, my Creator, I am totally dependent on you.
Everything is a gift from you.
All is gift.
I give thanks and praise for the gifts of this day. . . .
+
Help me:
Lord, I believe you work through and in time
to reveal me to myself. Please give me an
increased awareness of how you are guiding
and shaping my life, as well as a more
sensitive awareness of the obstacles I put in your way.
+
I love you:

You have been present in my life today.
Be near, now, as I reflect on:
Your presence in the events of today.
Your presence in the feelings I experienced today.
Your call to me.
My response to you.
+
Forgive me:
God, my creator, I ask your loving forgiveness and healing.
The particular incident of this day that I most want healed
is. . . .
+
Be with me:
Filled with hope and a firm belief in your love
and power, I entrust myself to your care and strongly
affirm. . . .[4]

For Your Personal Growth

Questions for reflection:

1. Do you think that in some ways, in certain situations, your energy is being drained by your negative attitudes? Is your energy being drained by the negativity of others?

2. If your energy is being drained by negativity, what are some positive actions you can take to correct that loss of energy and to be protected from and healed of its effects?

3. Reflect on your attitudes, memories, and beliefs that may precipitate negativity. Visualize yourself releasing those attitudes, memories, and beliefs.

Exercises:

1. Remember a time when you experienced the "spark of your soul." Recall how it reassured you of God's love for you.

2. Consider using the five steps of the Examen of Consciousness as a way of reflecting on your day and as a way of living your spiritual ideals more fully. Practice it consistently for a month to see if its ongoing practice brings balance and insight to your life as a stepmother.

NOTES

1. Caroline Myss, *Anatomy of the Spirit: The Seven Stages of Power and Healing* (New York: Harmony Books, 1996), 34–48.

2. Marian Cowan and John Carroll Futrell, *The Spiritual Exercises of St. Ignatius: A Handbook for Directors* (New York: Le Jacq Publishing, 1982), 33–35.

3. *"Homo Quidam Fecit Cenam Magnam,"* in J. M. Clark, *Meister Eckhart: An Introduction to the Study of His Works with an Anthology of His Sermons* (London: Thomas Nelson & Sons, 1957), 158–160, as quoted in Cowan and Futrell, 159.

4. Jacqueline Syrup Bergan and Marie Schwan, *Love: A Guide for Prayer* (Ijamsville, Md.: The Word Among Us Press, 2003), 19–20.

CHAPTER 9

Slow to Anger

I believe that anger and resentment are facts of life. And the reality is that, as stepmothers, we are especially vulnerable to these negative emotions. After all, we sometimes experience anger and resentment in our relationship with our biological children. So it is only to be expected that we should also experience these emotions in our interactions with our stepchildren, with whom our relationships may be less grounded and more prone to stress.

As stepmothers, we place extraordinary expectations on ourselves to bond with our stepchildren, to give ourselves totally to them, and to transcend all the negative stepmother myths. I suspect that most of our husbands unintentionally place similar expectations on us, not to mention the expectations that the children themselves may have. Unrealistic expectations set us up for disappointment and frustration.

Stepfamilies, at least initially, are extremely vulnerable and have many issues yet to resolve. Difficult and painful situations arise that can easily lead to hurt, anger, and resentment. Some people claim that when women marry men with children, their role is simply to be the children's friend. That may be true if the children are nearing adulthood, but if the children are young they need the care and love of a nurturing parent. Our task is to do the best we can, but not to expect perfection from our husbands, the children, or ourselves.

In his book *The 7 Habits of Highly Effective Families*, Stephen R. Covey observes that anger and other negative emotions are what most frequently get families off track. "Even if anger only surfaces one-tenth of one percent of the time, it will affect the quality of the rest of the time," he writes.[1] When a family member lashes out in uncontrollable rage, other family members experience fear, intimidation, and hurt. The result can be that everyone walks on eggshells in the hope of avoiding another outburst. Angry attacks tend to take the wind out of everyone's sails. Outbursts of anger defeat a family! No one feels free to authentically express himself or herself. Members of the family begin to separate from each other. Being a family is seen as too risky!

To commit oneself to stepmothering a child is a noble and beautiful aspiration, and one that is entirely attainable. However, it is essential to our well-being, and consequently to our growth in becoming a loving stepmom, that we recognize, own, and deal with our anger and resentment. The energy generated by a heart consumed with resentment can be destructive, can precipitate depression and illness, and can lead to various forms of codependent and abusive behaviors. Not only is our own well-being at stake, but so is the well-being of the entire family. We are too important to allow the powerful emotions of anger and resentment to fester and destroy us and our families. We must learn how to deal with these destructive feelings!

The most pernicious means of dealing with anger is to deny it. If we suppress and deaden our feelings of anger, we run the risk of deadening all our feelings. We can become walking zombies, wearing false smiles and spouting inauthentic gentility. Suppression of anger leads to paralysis of emotions and twisted outbursts. It can be the root of undefined, unexplainable anxieties. There is no alternative. We need to learn how to work with our anger so that we will not be controlled or destroyed by it.

I am amused when I look at the meaning of the words "anger" and "resentment" in the dictionary. Webster defines "anger" as "a strong feeling of displeasure and usually of antagonism." "Resentment" is defined as "a feeling of indignant displeasure or persistent ill will at something regarded as a wrong, insult, or injury." I can't speak for anyone else, but in my experience "strong displeasure" and "persistent ill will" don't even come close to capturing the real experience of anger. It is impossible to articulate the gamut of emotional reactions we experience as we perceive that we are being unjustly treated or misunderstood. The hurt, helplessness, and hopelessness of it defy definition and can trigger self-doubt and insecurities that lie hidden beneath the surface. Until we find ways to control our feelings of anger and resentment, we run the risk of letting our anger and resentment control us and our family.

Ways to Deal with Anger Constructively
The creation of a healthy stepfamily calls for a commitment to avoid saying or doing anything that will cause fear or pain to its members. It calls for a commitment to learn how to accept and deal with our anger in noncombative and constructive ways; it calls for putting an end to judging others; it calls for a moratorium on trying to change, "shape up," or manipulate others. Patience, persistence, and compassion are essential if we, as stepmothers, hope to create a healthy, happy stepfamily.

When faced with a situation that has the potential for hurt and anger, we have to be especially careful not to lose our "centeredness," that deep place within us where God dwells and continues to give us life and healing. We must cultivate an awareness of inner attitudes that make us vulnerable to hurt and anger. If we have the attitude that our stepchildren are out to get us or are untrustworthy and mean spirited, we are setting ourselves up for hostility, both in ourselves and from them. If, on the other hand, we cultivate an attitude that sees the basic goodness in them, we are much more able to see things from their perspective. A positive attitude can go a long way in dissipating stressful emotions. It's not that we allow ourselves to be treated disrespectfully or that we become overwhelmed by situations or outbursts from other family members. Instead, we choose to respond rather than to react. We choose to listen and empathize, to show compassion.

When I feel that I may respond to a situation with anger or hostility, I have found that the best "first response" is to walk away and give myself an opportunity to meditate and cool down. Children seem to respond pretty well when you say something like, "I'm feeling too angry to talk about this right now. I'm afraid I might say something I will regret." In addition to giving yourself some much-needed decompression time, you're modeling appropriate anger management behavior for your children.

In their book *How to Talk So Kids Will Listen and Listen So Kids Will Talk*, Adele Faber and Elaine Mazlish discuss effective ways to express and respond to feelings such as anger.[2] When we are angry, we want others to acknowledge and care about the way we feel. Yet there is little chance that they will empathize with us if we heatedly blame them or take out our feelings on them. Instead, we need to *explain* how the incident or action has made us feel. Suppose I were to walk into my stepdaughter's room and see my best pair of earrings on her dresser. I could immediately hunt her down and scream, "I can't believe you took my earrings without asking me! Don't you have any consideration for other people's property?" More than likely she will scream back at me, and our interchange will escalate from there. On the other hand, what if I were to wait for a time when both of us could be alone, and then say, "When I saw my earrings on your dresser this morning, I felt like my privacy had been violated—like when you see your sister wearing your new sweater without asking you. I love the fact that you want to borrow my jewelry. Just ask me first next time, okay?" By approaching her this way, I will have the satisfaction of expressing my feelings, and my stepdaughter is much less likely to feel like she has been attacked. I will have helped to build our relationship rather than to tear it down.

By understanding how we want others to respond to our feelings, we can better understand how to respond to theirs. A helpful way to respond to our children's anger is to acknowledge and empathize with how they feel, using words like, "I can see now that what I did really hurt your feelings. I wish I had done things differently." It isn't easy to stay calm when children are screaming at you, as angry children often will. But if, instead of screaming back, we can try to understand the way they feel, we will help dissipate their anger and perhaps pave the way for fruitful problem-solving discussions.

I recall two situations involving anger that happened with a grown stepchild. In the first incident, when negative things were said about me, I cried and defended myself profusely. That only made matters worse. My husband was then drawn into the fracas, and another layer of emotion was added. It was a terrible scene. I ended up a whimpering mess, and it took me several days to recover. It no doubt took my husband and stepchild a long time to recover, too.

In the second situation, resentment was expressed toward me for things I did and did not do that were perceived as "not being of a good heart." In that instance I was more centered and responded with compassion. I saw that my stepchild was making an honest effort to tell me about her feelings of pain and resentment. I felt sadness that my stepchild had carried such a heavy load of resentment for so many years and was still burdened with it. I saw that a great deal of suffering had resulted from my marrying my husband and entering my stepchild's home and family.

I was graced at the moment to admit and take responsibility for the fact that there were many times when I reacted in a negative, hurtful way and was not nurturing, kind, or caring. I asked for forgiveness for those times. I offered a mild defense: I was only thirty-three at the time of the marriage, and there were many times when I was totally overwhelmed during those early years. The conversation closed with my stepchild saying, "I know you did the best you could, but I was very hurt by some of the things you did." In the second situation we both maintained our integrity; we were left with something to build on. I felt there was a real chance for reconciliation and healing. I am grateful that my stepchild had the courage to share her perceptions and feelings with me. There are still conversations that go awry, but we are all learning; we are sincere in our efforts and are headed in the right direction.

In order to respond in a mindful and compassionate manner to intense emotional situations, I have found that I must be faithful to a daily routine of prayer and meditation. The more stressful the situation, the greater the priority I give to my daily meditation. I don't manage well without it.

Jon Kabat-Zinn, in his book *Full Catastrophe Living: Using the Wisdom of Your Body and Mind to Face Stress, Pain, and Illness*, teaches a breathing awareness meditation that I have found to be helpful.[3] My discovery is that just being in the present moment, totally nonstriving and nonjudgmental, breathing in and breathing out the breath that gives me life, calms and grounds me. Our breath can be an incredibly powerful friend to us; it anchors our awareness in the rhythmic, flowing life process of our bodies. The simple practice of being aware of our breathing has an amazing potential to empower us to meet life's challenges with a peaceful, calm, mindful spirit. Dr. Kabat-Zinn recommends practicing this breathing meditation for at least twenty minutes each day.

For centuries spiritual masters have taught the importance of breathing as a way of drawing near to God. Praying with attentiveness to our breath is akin to what is known as centering or contemplative prayer. Although it may take some practice to feel comfortable with praying in this way, there is nothing complicated about it. The more natural the breath, the better. Breathing from deep within the abdomen rather than from the upper chest facilitates this prayer and quiets the mind so that the person may be centered—that is, still and quiet within, open and receptive to the Holy Spirit's transforming action. A posture that maintains a straight spine is also helpful.

Because it is difficult to quiet our minds and racing thoughts, the masters suggest that we count our inhalations and exhalations or say a very simple monosyllabic word, such as peace or love, with each breath. Slowly our minds, bodies, and spirit will be quieted, and we will discover our deepest selves at rest in the presence of God. It takes some patience and discipline to pray in this manner, but the grace received is immeasurable; the centered quietness experienced in the prayer time will spill over into our daily activities. Our truest self is given life in this prayer.[4]

A wide range of options is available for dealing with feelings of anger and resentment. In the last few years I have discovered and grown to treasure the writings of Thich Nhat Hanh, a monk from Vietnam.[5] One method he suggests for dealing with difficult feelings is to recognize, name, greet, and speak with them:

"Hello fear, hello resentment.
I see you've come to pay me a visit.
We will have to walk together for a while.
You sit there, and I'll sit here and we'll look at each other."

I find if I recognize difficult feelings, they lose some of their power over me. Speaking to them has the effect of dissipating the negative energy. Harboring negative emotions only serves to exacerbate them.

In his book *Inner Work*, noted author Robert A. Johnson introduces a way of using our imagination to help resolve difficult emotions. It is called active imagination.[6]

Imagination is related to faith, and when we use it we can go deeper into ourselves to recognize what God is doing in us and in our lives. Active imagination helps us make that journey into ourselves. One way of using active imagination to resolve difficult emotions is to have a written conversation with the emotion or image that is troubling us. If we were to engage in active imagination with the emotion of resentment, it might look something like this:

Me:
Oh, here you are again! I'm feeling angry, filled with resentment. How could she have lied to me again? All I ever get from her is deception. Now I have to deal with this blasted anger. Resentment, what do you have to say for yourself? Why don't you leave me alone?

Resentment:
I don't like you much either. Did you think I really want to hear your whining again!

Me:

I have every reason to whine! How would you like it if someone you were making every effort to trust lied to you over and over?

Resentment:

I guess that's where I come in. If you let me stay, I'll fester within you and make you sick and then you can go to bed, or I can make your face get all wrinkled up with hate lines. What's your choice?

I have found that a written conversation with a difficult emotion nearly always results in a resolution. It may not happen on the first try, but repeated efforts are usually successful.

Composing a letter to the person you feel anger or resentment toward can also be helpful in diffusing those feelings, whether or not you ever actually deliver the letter. Writing your feelings down forces you to think them through completely and can help you decide on the best way to communicate them to the other person. You may also be surprised to discover that expressing your feelings on paper releases tension and can actually make your anger and resentment feel less severe.

Another way of using our imagination to bring difficult emotions to a resolution is to try to draw or paint them. What image captures the feeling? What color most represents it? Some people use clay to express and deal with feelings. Some write poetry or create stories. All of these ways of entering into our imagination have the potential of bringing forth images that will restore our serenity. Frequently when we use active imagination, symbols from deep within us may come forward, such as fire, water, or light, for example. Many of these symbols may resonate with the sacramental life we know and love in the church. These symbols can be powerfully reconciling.

I have found that using my imagination to deal with difficult feelings has been very helpful. This is especially true of resentment. At one point when things in our family were exceptionally difficult, I became nearly overwhelmed with resentment. I walked around like a festering boil, waiting to explode. I had been trying to resolve it for several weeks and had finally decided to see a therapist, who suggested that I see an art therapist on her staff. I had never heard of art therapy and had no idea what to expect. I was given a palette of paints and told to paint my resentment. That was all the instruction I got. It was all I needed. The paint flew! I couldn't get it onto the paper fast enough. The colors seemed to take on a life of their own. The images reeled forth like a film in fast-forward. After about an hour I felt totally drained. When the group was invited to share their "drawings" with each other, I was unable to do so. I was too tired! I went home exhausted, but I went home free! The demon of resentment had been released. I was amazed at what I drew and how it purged my emotions and helped me heal.

Imagination is an extraordinarily powerful gift. Its power can be frightening, and even disorienting. I want to give a word of caution about its use. The sudden release of a difficult emotion or hurt that you have suppressed over an extended period of time can be extremely unsettling. The new awareness that floods your consciousness can be difficult to assimilate. If you are dealing with severe pain or long-term suppression, I suggest that before engaging in active imagination you have someone available who can help you process your experience, such as a therapist or a spiritual director.

Our very lives depend on the way we deal with our anger and resentment. Research indicates there is a correlation between suppression of anger and certain diseases such as breast and lung cancer. Kabat-Zinn writes:

Studies support the notion that our physical health is intimately connected with our patterns of thinking and feeling about ourselves and also with the quality of our relationships with other people and the world. The evidence suggests that certain patterns of thinking and certain ways of relating to our feelings can predispose us to illness. Thoughts and beliefs that foster hopeless and helpless feelings; a sense of loss of control; hostility and cynicism toward others; a lack of commitment and enthusiasm about life's challenges; an inability to express feelings; and social isolation appear to be especially toxic. On the other hand, other patterns of thinking, feeling, and relating appear to be associated with robustness and health. People who have a basically optimistic perspective, who have the ability to "let go" of a bad event, who can see that it is impermanent and that their situation will change, tend to be healthier than their pessimistic counterparts.[7]

We all want to choose health; we want to choose life!

We can deal with our resentment and anger in creative ways; we can have enriching and rewarding relationships with our stepchildren. The desire and inspiration to love our family has its source and is rooted in God's love for us.

The LORD is gracious and merciful,
  slow to anger and abounding in steadfast love.
The LORD is good to all,
  and his compassion is over all that he has made.
(Psalm 145:8-9)

For Your Personal Growth

Questions for reflection:

1. How aware are you of what triggers your anger and resentment? What can you do to heighten that awareness?

2. Do you give yourself enough credit for the good you do?

3. Do you have unrealistic expectations that may be causing you stress and disappointment?

4. Have you set boundaries and limits that are respectful and essential to your well-being?

5. Is it possible that you take things too personally at times?

6. Are there certain perceptions and attitudes you might change in order to be more fully open and compassionate to your stepchildren? How can you make these changes?

7. In what ways is your anger a gift, moving you to action?

Scripture:

Let these words of St. Paul speak to your heart:

So then, putting away falsehood, let all of us speak the truth to our neighbors, for we are members of one another. Be angry but do not sin; do not let the sun go down on your anger. (Ephesians 4:25-26)

NOTES

1. Stephen R. Covey, *The 7 Habits of Highly Effective Families* (New York: Golden Books, 1997), 221.

2. Adele Faber and Elaine Mazlish, *How to Talk So Kids Will Listen and Listen So Kids Will Talk* (New York: HarperCollins, 1999).

3. Jon Kabat-Zinn, *Full Catastrophe Living: Using the Wisdom of Your Body and Mind to Face Stress, Pain, and Illness* (New York: Dell Publishing, 1990).

4. Gregory Mayers, *Listen to the Desert: Secrets of Spiritual Maturity from the Desert Fathers and Mothers* (Liguori, Mo.: Liguori/Triumph, 1996), 21–31.

5. Thich Nhat Hahn, *The Blooming of a Lotus: Guided Meditation Exercises for Healing and Transformation* (Boston: Beacon Press, 1993).

6. Robert A. Johnson, *Inner Work: Using Dreams & Creative Imagination for Personal Growth and Integration* (San Francisco: Harper & Row, 1986).

7. Kabat-Zinn, 216.

CHAPTER 10

Am I the "Wicked" Stepmother?

Is there anyone who doesn't know who Snow White is? And is there anyone who doesn't know that her stepmother is wicked?

Anyone who thinks that there's nothing in a name has never been called a "stepmother." As children, we were raised on fairytale images of evil stepmothers who cared only for themselves and their biological children and who plotted to do away with their stepchildren. As a young stepmother I felt the burden of those negative connotations, and was fearful of their influence on my stepchildren. I could easily identify with Hester Prynne in Nathaniel Hawthorne's literary masterpiece, *The Scarlet Letter*. Hester, a young woman in Puritan Massachusetts, gave birth to an illegitimate child and was forced by her revengeful husband to wear a scarlet "A" on her dress as punishment for adultery. I felt like I had a big red "W" on my dress. By the very fact that I was called a stepmother, I felt that I was being prejudged.

Of course, I was overreacting! I was a sensitive, thirty-three-year-old woman in a new marriage, in a new community, with five new stepchildren! I wanted desperately to build a new life and to be a positive, loving presence for the children. And I wanted desperately to show my new family that I wasn't wicked!

I am sure I am not alone in reacting to the negative connotations of the term "stepmother." I suspect that for most stepmoms it is a heavy burden to carry.

A Fairy Tale Existence

The issue, however, is complex and certainly not black and white. It is true that fairy tales have perpetuated the notion of the wicked stepmother. And it was a relief for me to discover that the very fairy tales with which we are so familiar were "edited" along the way to make them more palatable to children and adults by replacing malicious biological mothers with stepmothers. When I learned this piece of information, I was so excited that I immediately phoned my friends with the news! "Guess what," I told them, "the stepmothers were not wicked after all! Cinderella's stepmother was really her mother." Unfortunately, however, the image of the wicked stepmother has some grounding in reality. Studies show higher rates of child abuse and maltreatment in families in which there is a stepparent.

The most familiar stepmother tales in our culture are "Snow White and the Seven Dwarfs," "Cinderella," and "Hansel and Gretel." But many cultures have their own "wicked stepmothers." In one tale from Siberia, the wicked stepmother is turned into an owl to scare all the little children on dark nights.[1] In a Slavic tale, a little girl who lives with her stepmother and stepsister is made to do all the work.[2]

The simplicity and poignancy of fairy tales appeal to every age and generation. Despite historical and culture differences, fairy tales contain an element of universality and timelessness that resonates with each of us. Most have originated from tribal lore or folktales that were told in community gatherings and handed down from generation to generation. They were told in an adult setting and were intended for an adult audience.

Fairy tales are now regarded primarily as children's literature—although experts disagree about their suitability for children. Some scholars and psychologists believe that fairy tales can be therapeutic for children and enable them to understand their own life conflicts. Other specialists in child development maintain that tales in which children are victimized and characters are demonized can instill distrust, fear, and timidity. Even though the telling of a tale does not have the compelling power of a motion picture, the hearing of events such as being abandoned in the deep, dark woods; being shoved into an oven; or being eaten by a mean witch can scare almost anyone!

When considering fairy tales, it is important to realize that some tales do not authentically represent the original oral tradition. Modifications or embellishments not originally intended by the community have been introduced over time into many of these tales. That is what happened to the fairy tales we have inherited from the brothers Grimm.

Around 1810 Jacob and Wilhelm Grimm set about the daunting task of compiling the folktales of their German heritage. In their first edition they made an effort to be faithful to the original tales. The resulting volume, based on the unwieldy oral tradition, was long and scholarly, did not appeal to a large readership, and was criticized as unsuitable for children.

Sensitive to those criticisms and eager to promote sales, the brothers began to delete certain elements and exaggerate others. "The brothers no longer insisted on literal fidelity to oral traditions, but openly admitted that they had taken pains to delete 'every phrase unsuitable for children.'"[3] Their tales became so far removed from the oral tradition that they could not be considered literary folktales.[4]

The images and symbols in fairy tales are often referred to as "archetypes"—which the famous psychologist Carl Jung defined as "universal human characteristics which are inclined to produce the same or similar ideas in all people."[5] For example, everyone, no matter what their culture, knows what a witch is or has a mental picture of a monster.

One of the most significant of all archetypes is the mother. The positive aspects of the mother archetypes are those that nurture, cherish, give birth, promote growth, and provide sympathy and comfort. But the negative side of the mother archetype is just the opposite: darkness, secrecy, and whatever poisons, devours, or seduces. In fairy tales, it was easier for both children and adults to tolerate the idea of a wicked stepmother than a cruel biological mother. The stepmother could conveniently represent this negative side of the mother archetype.

So the wicked biological mother in Hansel and Gretel who suggested leaving her children in the forest to die became a stepmother in the Grimms' fourth edition. The wicked biological mothers of Snow White and Cinderella also became stepmothers. "In surveying the Grimms' collection of tales, it becomes clear that stepmothers and cooks are almost always thinly disguised substitutes for biological mothers."[6] In the *Dictionary of Symbols and Imagery*, Ad de Vries affirms the substitution of stepmothers for biological mothers when he defines the stepmother as "the Terrible Mother, masked."[7]

Is it any wonder that stepmothers are viewed so negatively in our culture? The Grimms' tales have been the pabulum of our children. The wicked stepmother in Walt Disney's production of *Cinderella* will continue to victimize her stepdaughter before endless generations of impressionable children! It's difficult to imagine the damage perpetrated on stepfamilies by the ubiquitous wicked stepmothers of the Grimms' collection of fairy tales.

Fortunately, not all fairy tales portray stepmothers in this negative light. One such example is an ancient tale from Iceland, "The Tale of Hildur," about a good stepmother. And not all writers of fairy tales used the wicked stepmother as a character. Ludwig Bechstein expressed his concern in 1856 about the projection of evil onto stepmothers when he wrote in the preface to his *New Book of German Fairy Tales,* "Among the thousands of children who every year get their hands on books of fairy tales, there must be many so-called stepchildren. When such a child—after reading many a fairy tale in which stepmothers appear—feels that it has been somehow injured or insulted by its own stepmother, then that young person makes comparisons and develops a strong aversion to its guardian."[8]

More recently, a children's book entitled *The Not So Wicked Stepmother,* by Leslie A. Venable, tells the story of two little girls and the emotional trauma they experience when their parents divorce. The girls share their story of how they came to love and respect their stepmother, Ashley, whom they discovered is different than they anticipated. Much to their amazement, she was not wicked at all![9] Today, when so many families are blended or binuclear, such stories help to empower and heal stepfamilies.

The Unfortunate Reality

While there is no doubt in my mind that fairy tales have, indeed, negatively influenced our perception of stepmothers, they nevertheless reflect an extremely disturbing reality. Children of stepfamilies—that is, families of one genetic parent and one stepmother or stepfather—"incur massive increases in the rates of the most severe forms of child maltreatment," according to researchers Martin Daly and Margo Wilson of McMaster University in Ontario. They claim, based on the studies they have compiled, that "having a stepparent has turned out to be the most epidemiological risk factor for severe child mistreatment yet discovered."[10]

The authors cite studies conducted in Great Britain, Canada, Australia, and Finland in which "stepparents were hugely overrepresented as perpetrators of registered child abuse and murders."[11] Even after variable risk factors such as poverty were calculated, the risks to stepchildren were "both genuine and huge."[12] Stepfathers outnumbered stepmothers in abuse and murder of their stepchildren, but there are more stepfathers than stepmothers, and the authors estimated that "the hazards are roughly comparable."[13] As for the causes of this abuse, the authors as well as other experts they quote point to the exceptional dynamics of stepparenting that involve so much opportunity for conflict.

Daly and Wilson's study focused on reported physical abuse. We can only speculate about the prevalence of unreported physical abuse as well as verbal and other more subtle forms of abuse. As a culture we must address the disgrace of this abuse, which is perpetrated by the minority. At the same time we must do all we can to help the increasing number of stepparents meet the enormous challenges of parenting their stepchildren.

There are, to be sure, many pitfalls in a stepfamily situation. The majority of stepparents, though, are not abusive and are making a supreme effort to parent their stepchildren in ways that are generous and humane. Although the bond between stepparent and stepchild may be different from that between a parent and a genetic child, it is loving nonetheless and can bring fulfillment and enrichment to both parent and child.

Stepparenting is a noble task that merits the help and support of the entire human community. We need to put aside the stereotypical image of the stepmother as wicked and show appreciation for the monumental task she has undertaken in loving another woman's child.

The "Wicked" Stepmother in Ourselves

We all have the potential for good and for evil. This struggle manifests itself in all aspects of our lives, including the way we mother our stepchildren. Sometimes, like St. Paul, we do the good we intend to do, and sometimes we do the very things we hate and do not intend to do. Sometimes we act like the good stepmother, and sometimes we act like the not so good, perhaps even wicked, stepmother.

That doesn't mean that we *are* wicked stepmothers. It means that, like all human beings, we have the potential for both good and evil within us. That knowledge need not discourage us, because as St. John beautifully reassures us in his gospel, the light of Christ is greater than the darkness, and this light is our heritage: "[A]nd the life was the light of all people. The light shines in the darkness, and the darkness did not overcome it" (John 1:4-5).

Ironically, if our light is to shine to its potential, we must become more aware of the dark. If we fail to recognize and acknowledge the wounded side of our human nature, we can frequently get ourselves into situations in which we have difficulty coping. And if we attempt to deny or repress our negative feelings, they may show up in sudden bursts of irrational behavior or anger. We have all known people who are really "nice" all the time and then suddenly explode. Unfortunately, none of us can maintain a pleasant exterior forever. I suspect that continuous repression of negative emotions is a significant factor in abusive situations when parents and stepparents lose all self-control. Women seem to be particularly prone to this "always wanting to please" behavior, which over time, can totally exhaust them and rob them of their normally excellent coping skills.

I recall an incident that occurred shortly after Leonard and I got married. It happened during the traumatic adjustment period, when

125

among other things, I was becoming acquainted with his longtime friends. We were attending a party one night when I overheard one of the women speak critically of me. She said, "She is way too nice! She can't possibly be real!" It was painful to hear her comment, but I had to admit that there was an element of truth in it. No doubt she had tuned in to the colossal effort I was making to be accepted during those first few months. If I had tried to maintain such a high degree of "niceness" for a prolonged period of time, I probably would have exploded. Certainly I would have become exhausted.

Gradually I learned to relax, but I can't seem to escape a tendency to try too hard to do too much and present a "nice" exterior. It is repressive and always leads to fatigue and less ability to cope. This tendency is not what I want and does not reflect my truest self. I think it comes from some place deep within me that does not recognize my own worthiness and is fearful of rejection. That place within may be a piece of my shadow.

Our "dark" side may also show itself by being the obstacle that stands between our good intentions and our actual accomplishments. It could be the energy behind our prejudices. Frequently, it is responsible for the projections we cast on other women. For instance, what we most dislike and condemn in those women may, in some measure, be representative of us. The good news is that a greater awareness of this "darker" side can be very enlightening and can even have a balancing and tempering effect on our behavior.

In the early years of our marriage, I remember feeling guilty if I was "lazy," by which I meant that I slept late, didn't finish every single household chore, or made Hamburger Helper for dinner. I considered laziness bad, but I didn't realize until later that it wasn't laziness that was my weakness, it was my obsession with accomplishing everything on the list I had made for myself. My so-called laziness actually saved me from pushing myself to the breaking point or becoming ill. In those days, I had a clear and somewhat rigid idea of what was good and what was bad. In retrospect I understand how what I thought at the time was bad may have been good. My inclination to be "lazy" actually protected me by tempering my compulsivity toward perfectionism.

Most people would consider the emotion of anger to be one of those attributes of our wounded nature. But as I look back, the anger I experienced ended up having an incredibly positive influence on the mothering of my children and stepchildren. When Leonard and I had been married for a few years, a certain type of self-destructive behavior erupted in our family. I became so furious at the participants that I wanted to wring their necks. So what could possibly be the light within such a dark emotion?

As it turns out, my anger actually offered me a great grace. Through my anger I was strengthened to make an assertive stand against what the members of my family were doing. They were not acting in their own best interest or in the best interest of the family. The force and energy of my anger mobilized me to do what I could to help them; it drove me to join with my husband in trying to get them the help they needed. Without such anger, I wouldn't have been compelled to take action to help them. And because my anger had a positive outlet, I didn't succumb to my desire to wring anyone's neck! I'm not always aware enough to tap into the light in dark situations, but I am grateful for those times when I am given the grace to do so. I ask for forgiveness for those times when I am not.

The challenge is to look deeply within, to recognize and own our potential for wickedness. We need to say to the "wicked" stepmother within us, "Yes, I know you are there. I know you are powerful. But do not forget that the power of light is stronger than the power of darkness. I will glean from you precious energy and strength." Our dark stepmother within may be cunning, but she need not win.

Ignorance is our enemy. Without the awareness that we have a strong energy of darkness residing in us, we stand the danger of becoming over-confident of our goodness. Then we will be unprepared for the snares of darkness that may come upon us suddenly. Triggered by certain insecurities or explosions against rigid repressions, we can be thrust into behaviors we never dreamed we were capable of. If I know I have the capability of becoming very angry, I can begin to counter it before it arises. If necessary, I can seek help in learning how to use it constructively. But if I deny my anger, my life can turn into a destructive series of temper tantrums.[14]

If we do not seek to understand the attributes of our wounded selves, we will not be empowered by the energy they produce in us; we become vulnerable and risk that this energy will be expressed destructively. Discerning what is good and what is not good, what is of God and what is not of God, is not as simple as it first appears. It can be difficult to recognize the subtle seductiveness of evil. However, we are not perfect, nor are we called to perfection. As we work toward spiritual and emotional maturity, we must increasingly depend on God. We need to remember and take comfort in the words of St. Paul, "'My grace is sufficient for you, for power is made perfect in weakness.' So, I will boast all the more gladly of my weaknesses, so that the power of Christ may dwell in me" (2 Corinthians 12:9).

For Your Personal Growth

Questions for reflection:
1. What, if any, prejudices did you have toward stepmothers before you became one?

2. Recall from your own childhood the fairy tales, myths, television shows, or movies in which stepmothers were portrayed. How did they shape your perception of stepmothers?

Exercise:
Take some time to pray through this exercise on light and darkness: [15]

In beginning this prayer, reflect on how utterly dependent you are on God's goodness and guidance. In the silence of your deepest self, declare your dependency on God.

I invite you to ask God to give you the wisdom to discern the darkness within yourself. Ask God to help you stand against the subtle and particular ways in which your dark shadow tempts you; ask for assistance in those areas in which you are most vulnerable. Ask God for the knowledge of a true life of goodness and the wisdom to make all your decisions in light of that goodness.

Consider the light and darkness, the good stepmother and the dark stepmother within you.

Keeping in mind that some of the snares the dark stepmother uses are fear, exaggeration, self-pity, self-doubt, and discouragement, ask yourself questions such as the following:

1. How does fear erode my trust in others, including my husband, my children, my stepchildren, and myself?

2. How does fear cause me to wear a mask that hides my true feelings, my weaknesses, and even my strengths from others?

3. How does fear of the unknown lead me to compulsively seek status or wealth?

There is incredible energy within our shadow selves. If we do not seek to understand it, we will not be empowered by it. We are vulnerable and risk our shadow energy's being expressed destructively if we remain ignorant of its power.

4. How does my exaggeration or understatement of self serve to manipulate people into praising me?

5. How does exaggeration cause me to over-evaluate myself and consequently to demand unjust recognition and recompense from my husband, family, friends, and others?

6. How does self-pity lead me to be critical and petty, and especially to be hypercritical of my family?

7. How does self-pity lead me to destructive negative thinking and denial of my talents and/or those of my family and others?

8. How does self-doubt push me to be pompous, that is, to be "front and center"?

9. How does self-doubt addict me to an insatiable appetite for perfection and affirmation?

10. How does self-doubt keep me from developing and exercising my talents?

11. How does a sense of discouragement lead me to under-achieve?

12. How does a sense of discouragement lead me to complain, whine, and make unrealistic demands of my husband and family as well as others?

13. Looking at the world on a global scale, how are people being controlled by these same evil tools through hero worship of "stars" or building weapons of destruction or rampant nationalism?

Considering that the good stepmother's approach is characterized by honesty, gratefulness, receptivity, and genuineness, reflect on the following questions to better grasp her influence:

1. How does the experience of gratitude for the gifts of the earth and for my talents free me from possessiveness and release me to share with my husband, children, stepchildren, and others?

2. How does gratefulness allow me to celebrate the achievements of self, family, and others?

3. How does being receptive open me to mutually trusting and transparent relationships, especially within my family?

4. How does openness release courage within me to dare to risk failure and rejection, particularly in the complexities of my binuclear family?

5. How does openness free me to acclaim the gifts of others, especially the developing talents and gifts of the children in our stepfamily?

6. How does honesty free me to recognize my own limitations and to welcome constructive criticism from others?

7. How does honesty release me from cheating others of what they are entitled to?

8. How does honesty free me to recognize the needs of others, especially the heightened needs of the children in our binuclear family?

9. How does honesty release me from inflation of self or from expecting too much of others or myself?

10. How does genuineness free me from overstriving so that I may live in a spirit of contentment with what I have and with what I can comfortably accomplish?

11. How does genuineness release me from holding myself aloof from others, especially from my stepchildren?

12. On a global scale, how do I see nations and peoples being freed by embracing the qualities of the good stepmother, for example, through openness to life, care of our planet, programs to relieve hunger, and the like?

I invite you to close your reflection by asking Mary, the mother of Jesus, to intercede for you. Ask Mary, the mother of us all, to empower you through the Holy Spirit to be the light of goodness to your husband, children, and stepchildren. May you be given the grace to put all your talents, possessions, and achievements at the service of God. Finally I invite you to request the Creator of all goodness to continue to embrace and enliven you with courage, love, and peace.

Scripture:

In solidarity with each other, may all of us as stepmothers be released into the joy of the gifts of God's own Spirit, the gifts St. Paul speaks of in his Letter to the Galatians:

[T]he fruit of the Spirit is love, joy, peace, patience, kindness, generosity, faithfulness, gentleness, and self-control. There is no law against such things. (Galatians 5:22-23)

It is in receiving the gifts of the Spirit that the authentic beauty of ourselves as women, as wives, as mothers, and as stepmothers will be reflected.

Take joy! We are, after all, quite lovely and fair!

NOTES

1. Emery Bernhard, *The Girl Who Wanted to Hunt: A Siberian Tale* (New York: Holiday House, 1994).

2. Beatrice Schenk de Regniers, *Little Sister and the Month Brothers* (retelling) (New York: Lothrop, Lee & Shephard Books, 1967).

3. Maria Tatar, *The Hard Facts of the Grimms' Fairy Tales* (Princeton: Princeton University Press, 1987), 19.

4. Tatar, 33.

5. C. G. Jung, trans., R. F. C. Hull, *Four Archetypes: Mother, Rebirth, Spirit, Trickster* (Princeton: Princeton University Press, 1967), 5.

6. Tatar, 144.

7. Ad de Vries, *Dictionary of Symbols and Imagery* (Amsterdam: North-Holland Publishing Company, 1984), 442.

8. Tatar, 142.

9. Leslie Allgood Venable, *The Not So Wicked Stepmother: A Book for Children and Adults* (Birmingham: L. A. Venable Publishing, 1998).

10. Martin Daly and Margo Wilson, *The Truth about Cinderella, A Darwinian View of Parental Love* (New Haven: Yale University Press, 1998), 58.

11. Daly and Wilson, 32.

12. Daly and Wilson, 28.

13. Daly and Wilson, 60–61.

14. Please see Chapter 9, "Slow to Anger," where I discuss various ways of dealing with anger.

15. This prayer reflection is an adaptation of the Two Standards from the *Spiritual Exercises of St. Ignatius*.

CHAPTER 11

Just You and Me, Babe

A loving relationship between a husband and wife bestows a sense of security and safety to the entire family. If this is true for a nuclear family, it is all the more true for a binuclear family in which the children as well as the adults have had the very foundation of their lives shaken by divorce or death. Everyone enters into the newly created family with trepidation and fear. A sense of security can, in large measure, be restored when the children see their mother or father loving and being loved, happy in their marriage. Children naturally feel safe in a home where love is present.

"Just you and me, Babe! These kids will grow up, have lives of their own, and then it will be just you and me." These words from my husband reassured me in difficult times. They spoke of his love for me and of his trust in our love. In effect, he was saying to me, "We love each other, and we will stand together no matter what happens. Our love *will* survive." I cannot begin to count the times those words saved me from feeling completely overwhelmed.

The words "Just you and me, Babe" are meant not to imply exclusivity but to establish priority. The phrase doesn't mean that we don't love or care for our children, but rather that we recognize that our married relationship is central to our family's success and well-being. I feel strongly that the greatest gift a couple can give their children is to love one another.

Thirty-two years have passed since Leonard first spoke those words to me, and we are still here, still loving each other. The children did grow up, and they do have lives of their own. Just as we did, they also are experiencing the joys and struggles of adult life circumstances and commitments. They too are choosing priorities, deciding to whom or to what they will be forever faithful.

We were married on a beautiful autumn evening, on the last day of November 1972, in the Cathedral of the Immaculate Conception. It was a very simple ceremony, with only our children, my sister, and one close friend present. I feel the same thrill I felt that night when I remember how handsome and strong Leonard looked in his striking gray suit. I could hardly take my eyes off of him. My heart sang; I felt as if I were the most blessed woman in the world. The children looked beautiful, dressed in their best clothes. I wonder now what their young hearts held. Were they excited, fearful? I suspect they were bewildered.

Our wedding flowers consisted of one small green plant offered by my youngest child, James. This plant, we explained to our children, was to symbolize the newness of our life together. Throughout the years I have frequently thought of that small green plant. What nourished its growth? What cost did its growth exact? How does it now symbolically represent what we have become as a family?

Two years ago we had a family portrait taken to celebrate our thirtieth wedding anniversary. The photographs were splendid, so splendid that I was moved to tears of deep gratitude and honest pride. We have not evolved into a perfect couple or a perfect family, but we have grown and have been transformed like good wine into our own unique and precious family.

Love does that! It transforms. I love the story of Jesus transforming the water into wine at the wedding at Cana (John 2:1-11). The Scripture passage speaks of God's miraculous ongoing creation.

God gave birth to love two thousand years ago when Christ was born, and God continues to bring love into the world. The man and woman who pledge their lives to each other, who promise to love each other unconditionally and without measure, are a sign of God's birth of love; by saying yes to each other they participate in God's labor of love. The actions and activities of their ordinary daily lives are the fruition and revelation of the extraordinary love God has for all of us.[1] The wine of the joy a married couple share spills over abundantly to their family, to their friends, and to the extended community; the energy of their love is limitless, its creative influence far greater than they could ever dream or imagine.

The poet E. E. Cummings speaks of the boundlessness of love:

love is a place
& through this place of
love move
(with brightness of peace)
all places

yes is a world
& in this world of
yes live
(skillfully curled)
all worlds[2]

Who could resist saying yes to such love? I couldn't! "Arise, my love, my fair one, and come away" (Song of Solomon 2:10).

It is a strong call, this love. Make no mistake: Marriage is hard, tough work! Marriage is a difficult undertaking for any couple, but for the couple that has children from a previous marriage, it is an incredible challenge that stretches and stresses every ounce of love they can possibly muster. The wine of happiness that my husband and I experience with each other and our family has come to fullness through a long process of fermentation. In the effervescence of the chaotic early years of our marriage, there were many times, I am sure, that my husband did not think of me as his fair one. Nor did I always remember how my heart sang at our wedding. No, there were times when the wine was pretty sour, more like vinegar! That is all part of the creative process. Being faithful and attentive to the process is essential.

Good marriages, like good wine, do not just happen. They require patience, focus, planning, energy, and effort. The cornerstone of a happy marriage is for the couple to be each other's best friend. It is essential that we, as wives, do our part to nurture that friendship. Our task is to keep our hearts and minds focused and committed to the goal of loving our husbands. We need to put forth substantial effort and energy into getting to know him at the deepest level: What makes him happy? What are his dreams? Of what is he most proud? What does he most regret?[3]

My husband is big, strong, wise, and successful. Initially, it was difficult for me to imagine that he needed anything. That was a false assumption! Although I do not see myself as a wise old sage, one thing I have definitely learned is that a husband needs his wife's approval, appreciation, admiration, encouragement, and most of all her trust. He needs to know he is her knight in shining armor!

Faithful attentiveness creates a happy marriage, and couples that are combining families from previous marriages can be confident of its rewards. Author Barbara Mullen Keenan reassures us, "The marriage which blends two families may be more complex and difficult than a marriage that is unencumbered with responsibilities from the past, but it has every potential of being just as fulfilling."[4]

God as Our Anchor

How does one hold on to the dream, and find the energy to be faithful while immersed in the unyielding daily struggle of a marriage that has united two separate families? How can one keep responding to the call of love's embrace?

There is a boundless empowering source of love, grace, and blessings deep within us that is always present, always available, waiting to be released into the world; it is in the deepest center core within us where God dwells, where we are one in God and one in God's love. The spiritual master Meister Eckhart expresses his experience of God's indwelling this way: "It is here that God's foundation is my foundation, and my foundation is God's." He asks the question, "What does it mean to share a foundation with God? It means . . . entering into our truly free nature."[5] Grounded in this primary source of love, our truest selves are freed and strengthened to love as God loves, unencumbered, unconditionally.

Our authentic response to love's call is dependent on our desire to be faithful and steadfast in our openness to God's love within us. God will acknowledge our prayer of desire and reward us with the spirit of love, increasingly spilling over into the activities and actions of our daily lives. James Finley, in his book *Christian Meditation: Experiencing the Presence of God*, states that the fruit of our fidelity to prayer is a growing awareness of God's abiding presence in all things:

> Consider a moment of spontaneous meditative awareness in which a woman sees her beloved. She holds her beloved. And in doing so she is awakened to a love which transcends the concrete immediacy of the beloved. By that I mean that the love to which she is awakened transcends whether or not his hair is combed, or even whether or

not he has any hair. The love she experiences transcends whether or not he is wearing matching socks. Every detail about him is transcended by the love to which his presence awakens her. . . . She is awakened to the mystery of love manifesting itself in and as who he simply is.[6]

To acquire this grace of awareness is, indeed, worth every effort and discipline necessary to nurture a life of faithful prayerfulness.

A stepfamily is like a huge living organism, each part dynamically affecting the whole. The relationships within any family are multiple, but in a stepfamily they are multitudinous. There is a great deal of energy whirling around, and it is easy to flail and thrash about wildly in its gusts of conflict and need. Our sanity as wives, mothers, and stepmothers is contingent upon our hearts being firmly centered in God. We dare not move from that center core of life within. When we sense that we have strayed from it, we need to return quickly; we need to return over and over to that core within that keeps us stable and true. People who travel by sea have learned the importance of an anchor. According to Meister Eckhart, "If they wish to sleep, they throw an anchor into the water so that the ship will come to a halt. Of course, they rock up and down on the water, but they do not move off."[7] That is the call of love: to stay anchored in God; everything else will revolve around that anchor.

I see my anchor as a triangle with God at the center and myself, my husband, and our children at the outer points. The tensile strength of the center holds the three points of the triangle in balance. Every binuclear family experiences intense relational pressures, and our young family was no exception. I am amazed when I recall my responses to various situations. When I was not still and centered within, things flew apart; but when I was anchored in God, my response was authentic, compassionate, and wise. The Spirit of God seemed to flow through me.

In the early months, even years, of our marriage, I struggled with my innate propensity to become overwhelmed. It seemed as if I was in a constant state of overload. Although my husband was loving and supportive, there were many times I felt alone and powerless. Denial was a major contributor to my sense of helplessness. I was forever getting snared in the myth that the binuclear family was just like every other "normal" family. I remember getting a harsh reality check a couple of years after our wedding. A close friend who is a marriage and family therapist corrected my image of our family. She said, "You have this portrait image of yourselves as a nuclear family: you and Leonard and the children. That is not how it is! It is you and Leonard in the middle, with his children on one side and your children on the other. You are not a nuclear family. It is wise to remember that." Val Farmer, clinical psychologist and columnist, also advises, "Give up your nuclear family myth of making this 'one happy family.' The only thing nuclear will be the explosions going off around you."[8]

To make matters worse, I was living in a new community without a network of support. I had entered the marriage as a very confident, independent, capable young professional woman and mother. But during those first few months, my self-esteem suffered severe erosion. I bristled every time I was introduced as or referred to as "Leonard's new wife." The community was welcoming, but the title "new wife" made me feel "second best," not as good as the wife that had preceded me. We need to be more sensitive to and supportive of women who marry men who have been married before. After all, "nearly one-third of all women who marry in any given year are second wives; 84 percent of those become stepmothers."[9]

The expectations placed on a woman who marries a man with children are excessive and usually carry the added complexity of being unspoken and vague. Frequently she simply does not understand what people want or need. More likely than not, she is driven by her desire to please everyone. She is rejected and resented when she is unable to meet expectations, and credit and thanks are not readily forthcoming for the times she does. It is a confusing dilemma!

Many women marrying a man with children find that those children are in great emotional turmoil, are extremely needy, and may even be engaged in behaviors that are harmful. Her husband may unknowingly exacerbate the problem by denying his children's behavior or by adopting a permissive, indulgent response to it. In addition, he may have his own set of issues from the past, which out of love for him, his wife may experience as another wound she must heal, another expectation to be met.

Faced with the quandary of expectations and duties, the newly married woman who is bringing her own children into the marriage may have to deal with loyalty issues regarding the time and energy she has left over for them. In light of the situation of loss or changes, her children may also be in turmoil, needy, or acting out. She, too, may have issues from the past that from time to time resurface for attention.

The problems are numerous, the expenditure of energy is immense, and the woman who feels she can handle everything is her own worst enemy. There is a danger that her confidence may motivate her to place unreasonable demands on herself. She could easily fall prey to the temptation of thinking that the success of her marriage and the happiness of the entire family rest on her shoulders alone. She sets herself up for exhaustion and disappointment.

Learning to Grow in Acceptance

Growing in acceptance and trust is closely linked to growing in understanding. If we are going to accept things as they are, then it follows that we must first become attentive to discovering *how* things are. We must attempt to understand ourselves and those we love as much as we are able without being invasive. There will always be things we simply cannot understand. To probe and over-analyze is counterproductive. There are some things we ought to overlook, forgive, and forget.

Sometimes, no matter how hard both spouses try, they may not be able to reach an agreement or even a compromise on an important issue. To do so might require either the husband or the wife to sacrifice something they hold very dear to them. Sometimes the only recourse is to agree to disagree, especially if the issue involves one of the children. It should not be taken personally. "A couple can decide to reconnect at a feeling level rather than disconnect at an issue level."[10]

Authentic acceptance begins with accepting our own limitations; no one can do everything or be everything to everyone. For me, that has sometimes meant being content with being discontented. I fail but do not give up. I do not always do my best, but I do what I can! As I have grown in acceptance, it is easier to understand why I am not able to do this or that particular thing or why I am vulnerable in certain situations. Acceptance means that I am honest about my dependency on God and my need to be anchored in God.

Leonard's and my understanding and acceptance of each other blossomed when, in October 1976, we attended Marriage Encounter. Marriage Encounter is a weekend retreat experience which, although Catholic in orientation, is open to couples of all faiths. It is an opportunity for couples to share their feelings, joys, fears, and frustrations in a safe environment. Couples are directed to dialog with each other on particular focused questions such as, In what area am I least open to listen to you? What feeling is most difficult for me to share? When do I feel closest to you? Marriage Encounter came at just the right time for us: We had been married for four years, were well past the honeymoon, and were dealing with serious family issues. We opened ourselves completely to the process and were richly rewarded. We used the opportunity to clarify issues, reconcile differences, and reach consensus on areas that were troubling. We shared our vulnerabilities and told each other how we wanted and needed to be listened to and loved. Most of all, we realized how deep our love was, how right we were for each other. God had been present in the very beginning, when we first found each other, and God would sustain us, no matter what happened. We knew that we would be given what we needed to meet the challenges of our marriage and family. We went home from our weekend affirmed and deeply committed to continue to grow in understanding, acceptance, and love.

The grace of our Marriage Encounter has continued to inspire me throughout our marriage. I have never lost sight of Leonard's words, "Just you and me, Babe." Each day I pray for our married love, pray that we grow in accepting and loving each other. I truly want to be a loving wife, to be a source of joy for my husband. We all do! The words of the prophet Sirach can serve to inspire us.

Happy is the husband of a good wife;
*   the number of his days will be doubled.*
A loyal wife brings joy to her husband,
*   and he will complete his years in peace.*
A good wife is a great blessing;
*   she will be granted among the blessings of the man*
*   who fears the Lord.*

Whether rich or poor, his heart is content,
and at all times his face is cheerful. . . .
Like the sun rising in the heights of the Lord,
so is the beauty of a good wife in her well-ordered home.
(Sirach 26:1-4, 16)

Those of us in a binuclear marriage need all the help we can get to even come close to being the loving wife Sirach exalts!

Strengthening Your Marriage Relationship

If you want to strengthen your marriage relationship, a good way to start is reading books by well-regarded psychologists and marriage therapists. As a young wife I was at a disadvantage, since I came from a dysfunctional family in which my mother and father vacillated between estrangement and ecstasy. I had not been raised in a family where there was a healthy, loving marriage, but I had always dreamed of being happily married. Having experienced failure in my first marriage, I was sincerely intent—even driven—to do whatever it took[11] to have a marriage that was fulfilling and happy for my husband and me, a marriage that would lovingly embrace all of our children. Aware of what I had missed in my childhood, knowing how little I knew, I was drawn to seek out books that could offer help.

There are many excellent authors, some of which have surfaced during the past few years. Two authors that I have found to be particularly valuable are Dr. John Gray and Dr. Phillip C. McGraw. (Their books are listed in the bibliography.) Both have made a remarkable contribution to couples intent on improving their relationships. I am very grateful to them for their insight and encouragement.

I found Dr. Gray's book *Men Are from Mars, Women Are from Venus* especially helpful. In it he explains the radical differences in the ways men and women think and leads couples to embrace their dissimilarities and discover the gifts hidden within them. I love the analogy that Dr. Gray uses when speaking of the intimacy pattern of men. He says that men are like rubber bands that stretch just so far and then withdraw. When they feel they are getting too close, they automatically pull back. I think it's safe to assume that most wives would agree! The dilemma, of course, is that our pattern of intimacy is very different from that of our husbands. We tend to be like waves reaching a peak and crashing down. That also rings true! The important thing is to realize that men are dissimilar from us, and their needs are distinctly different. The knowledge of the differences that exist between men and women can lead to greater understanding and acceptance in marriage. It helps to know what is going on! Once we know, we can make decisions about how to take care of ourselves, when to approach our husband, when to bring up difficult issues, and how to be most loving.[12]

The way men and women generally cope with stress is one of the biggest differences between them, since they process information differently. A man will usually withdraw (Dr. Gray describes this as a man going into his "cave"), while a woman usually prefers to talk her way through a stressful situation. This disparity can present a problem, but Gray advises women to accept their husband's temporary withdrawal and wait it out with as much graciousness as possible.[13]

Another author I hold in high esteem, May Sarton, writes of the high emotional cost an intimate, lasting relationship demands. She warns that its survival is impossible without the risk and pain of honest communication:

> Because passionate love breaks down walls and at first does it in a such a sovereign way, we are rarely willing

to admit how little that initial barrier-breaking is going to count when it comes to the slow, difficult, accepting of each other, when it comes to the irritations and abrasions, and the collisions, too, between two isolated human beings who want to be joined in a lasting relationship. So the walls go up again. The moment's vision is clouded, and mostly, I believe, by the fear of pain, our own and that of the other's, by the fear of rejection. To be honest is to expose wounds and also to wound. There is no preventing that. Union on a deep level is so costly that it rarely takes place. But withdrawal, censorship, the wish to keep the surfaces smooth because any eruptions spell danger and must therefore be prevented, is costly, too. Censorship simply drives conflict deeper inside. What is never discussed does not for that reason cease to exist. On the contrary, it may fester and finally become a killing poison.[14]

Sometimes talking is not the most loving way to communicate difficult feelings or negative emotions. When we are upset, we can say things that are not trusting and accepting; we can be judgmental, blaming, cause deep hurt, and alienate our husbands. It is wise to take time to cool off, to become centered again. In previous chapters, I have offered various ways of discerning and processing negative feelings. In my relationship with my husband, I have found writing down my feelings in a daily journal to be especially helpful. It has been an excellent way to gather my thoughts and clarify what I really think and need. It is never healthy to smother or deny our feelings. The intense energy of negative feelings, if unchecked, can consume our thoughts, dissipate our energy, and contaminate our efforts to be loving. Writing down our innermost feelings is a deliberate and prayerful endeavor that miraculously diffuses the energy of negativity so that positive feelings can enter our hearts again; it can prepare us to communicate with authentic forthrightness.

The Healing Power of Love Letters. A marvelous way to ask forgiveness or to express feelings of anger, resentment, sadness, or fear—as well as feelings of love—is to write your husband a love letter.

As women, we need to trust that our husbands really do love us, that they want to know how we feel and what we need to feel loved.[15] We have no right to be critical if we have not been honest about our feelings and have not asked for what we need. We cannot expect our husbands to read our minds and know our innermost needs. To be open and vulnerable is difficult, but progress is rarely made without taking risk. That is what is so marvelous about letter writing; it is easier and can serve as a preparation for face-to-face sharing. You may even choose to write a response letter from your husband in which he expresses what you want to hear. It may be wise to burn the letters that turn out to be a harsh venting of intense anger and judgment. I think of a harsh and mean letter as a "first-step" letter. When a letter is well thought out, reasonable and loving, a further step toward reconciliation can be to share it with your husband if, of course, you are comfortable doing so, and if, intuitively, it seems appropriate.

I am a believer in the healing power of love letters and have saved nearly all that I have received. Occasionally I give myself an extra boost by rereading them. A note that I especially treasure is one that my husband wrote to me shortly after we met. The freshness of his words, written thirty-two years ago, continues to be life giving; the promise and hope he wrote of still have the power to revitalize my love. Someone once spoke to me of the beauty and enduring quality of the written word. He said, "A spoken word of love is wonderful, but even a mild breeze can whisk it away. A written word of love is everlastingly precious."

The Importance of Sexual Intimacy. When we are in love, we instinctively yearn to know our beloved. The innermost essence, or heart knowledge, of who we are is revealed in sexual intimacy. Studies have shown that a healthy sexual relationship between a husband and wife who are deeply committed to each other is a major factor in having a happy marriage. Sex based on mutual trust and love has the ability to engender emotional closeness and warmth as well to give immense pleasure. Amazingly, the positive feelings it creates provide a couple with the experience of being passionate lovers as well as best friends. It also has an astonishing ability to heal and bridge chasms that may exist between them. The affirmation and emotional closeness that my husband and I experience through the sexual expression of our love always strengthens and creates more love. It gives me a sense of my worthiness to be loved and confirms me as the woman I am. "He loves me; he will always love me; this wonderful man loves me!" In the early years of our binuclear family, when stress was at its highest peak, sexual intimacy, I am sure, saved our sanity as well as our marriage. It was "a bridge over troubled waters"!

Sexual intimacy is integral and essential to matrimonial love. The vulnerability of sexual surrender not only reveals the inner beauty of our loved one to us, it transforms both husband and wife into greater beauty, into the image of God's own image. Sexual intimacy is the exciting magical component of marriage that bestows upon ordinary lives an extraordinary dimension of the sacred.

Unfortunately, there are a number of factors that can serve as a detriment to a fulfilling sexual relationship between a husband and wife. Perhaps the biggest culprit is, again, the basic differences between a man and a woman. Women and men are physiologically opposite. That is why we marry each other! It is also what makes harmonious sexual intimacy a challenge. Women experience far greater difficulty in achieving sexual satisfaction than men and have more problems than men sustaining an interest in sex. In his book *Kosher Sex*, Rabbi Shmuley Boteach attributes their difficulty directly to men who are not patient and "don't take time to romance the women they are with." He stresses that human sex is a "metaphor for God's creation of an interaction with the world." It "is an exalted form of communication" and "necessitates a focus on harmony and intimacy rather than mere pleasure or reproduction."[16] Mutually satisfying sexual intimacy requires that couples communicate freely with each other.

Obsession with sexuality in our culture makes it imperative that the gift and joy of sex be viewed through a spiritual perspective. Only that positive attitude will assure a lasting, fulfilling sexual relationship between husband and wife. We must assume responsibility for teaching our children that sex is a gift from God that is meant to create harmony and pleasure as well as babies. We must also rid ourselves of any misguided notions, perhaps founded on dated religious traditions, that sex is unholy. This attitude could foster a sense of prudishness, which can prevent us from freely loving our husbands or allowing them to love us.

Other detriments to healthy sexual expression are domination and dishonesty. Dishonesty, even in small things, has a devastating effect on a relationship. A husband or wife can rarely be deceived; each is deeply connected to his or her spouse and can detect, intuitively, deceit of the smallest degree. Lack of mutuality is similarly destructive. It is also imperative that mutuality exist in decision-making and in the disciplining of the children. While men have been traditionally accused of authoritarian domination, it is not only men who fall prey to it. Women also can be guilty of controlling and manipulative behavior. Without trust and mutuality, a marriage disintegrates. Dishonesty and domination herald the end of joy!

Joy is, however, readily available to the husband and wife who are attentive to respecting and reverencing each other and their vows. I have mentioned many ways in which a couple can nurture their pleasure and happiness in each other. Sometimes it is dependent on something as basic as being available, being rested, and not always scurrying around preoccupied with perfection. Care should also be taken to assure that, as busy and stressed parents in a stepfamily, we have quality time alone with each other. A young couple with a combined family of five children expressed how difficult this proved to be. "We just couldn't find time to be alone, to go out, to have fun and laugh together. We were always too tired for sex. We began to grow apart. In desperation, we made appointments for dates with each other."

Staying Attractive to Each Other. My husband told me that from the moment he first saw me, he knew I was meant for him. That is the voice of physical attraction! I suspect that most couples were initially drawn to each other by the physical magnetism they experienced. Physical attraction is important, not just in the beginning of a relationship, but even as we age. This is not a superficial observation. Physical attraction is a part of being human, and since God is revealed in us, it is also a part of being holy. Women love and need to be perceived as beautiful, and men want to be seen as irresistible.

Sometimes when the spark goes out of a marriage, the partners have simply stopped trying. We attend to every detail of our appearance when we are courting, because we care a great deal about how the object of our affections will perceive us. Yet years after we have been married, when we feel we no longer need to attract him, we sometimes have a tendency to let our appearance go. This is a mistake.

Don't get me wrong—I'm not saying that we should all have face lifts and tummy tucks or even dye our hair. Eventually both wife and husband will begin to go gray and sag—that's the beauty of growing old together. But regardless of our age, we can all do whatever we can to continue to look and be our best. That means exercising and eating right as well as staying well groomed and well dressed. Our grandmothers were taught to don a clean dress, fix their hair, and put on fresh makeup before their husbands got home from work. Life is very different now. For us, it may mean dressing in the kind of clothes our husbands like when we are together, rather than spending the day in sweats and slippers. Staying healthy and well groomed are ways that we care for the body that is God's gift to us. They are also gifts that we can continually give our spouses; for, in looking our best, we are showing that we care about them and want to please them. And isn't that what love is all about?

Our married lives are never static; there is a constant dynamic movement. At one point, energy will focus more directly on the married couple; at another time, a crisis with a child will require more attention. There may be occasions when an illness, extended family concerns, or a work-related issue demands a temporary extra amount of effort. Things are always changing, shifting back and forth between the points of the triangle of our lives. At particularly chaotic times, life can become overwhelming. God, however, is always creatively present in the love and effort a committed husband and wife share. If we surrender ourselves to each other and to God, our eyes will be fully opened to God's presence, and we will be firmly anchored in peace.

Thomas Merton speaks to us of God's enduring presence:

Life is simple.
We are living in a world that is absolutely transparent

and God is shining through it all the time.
This is not just a fable or a nice story.
It is true.
If we abandon ourselves to God
and forget ourselves,
we see it sometimes
and we see it maybe frequently.
God shows Godself everywhere,
in everything,
in people and in things and in nature and in events.
It becomes very obvious that God is everywhere and
in everything and we cannot be without God.
It is impossible.[17]

For Your Personal Growth

Questions for reflection:

1. Do you feel a need to better know your husband? If so, what options can you visualize to help you get to know him better?

2. Do you have a desire for your husband to know and understand you better? If so, discover ways to share yourself more fully with him. Can you see yourself writing him love letters in which you share your deepest self?

3. Do you and your husband have enough quality time together? If not, can you creatively rearrange your schedules to allow for it?

4. Are there areas in your marriage where you feel your needs or your husband's are not being met? If so, what plan of action can you put into place to meet these needs?

Activity:
Consider making a Marriage Encounter weekend.

Scripture:
Read the Song of Songs (Song of Solomon) from the Old Testament, and be amazed.

NOTES
_____

1. Matthew Fox, *Breakthrough: Meister Eckhart's Creation Spirituality in New Translation* (Garden City, N.Y.: Image Books, 1980), 61.

2. E. E. Cummings, *Collected Poems* (Franklin Center, Pa.: The Franklin Library, 1977), 271.

3. Phillip C. McGraw, *Relationship Rescue: A Seven Step Strategy for Reconnecting with Your Partner* (New York: Hyperion, 2000), 124–125, 138–139.

4. Barbara Mullen Keenan, *When You Marry a Man with Children: How to Put Your Marriage First and Stay in Love* (New York: Simon & Schuster, 1992), 22.

5. Fox, 203.

6. James Finley, *Christian Meditation: Experiencing the Presence of God* (New York: HarperCollins, 2004) 48.

7. Fox, 377.

8. Val Farmer, "Stepfathers Must Get Off to the Right Start," *Pioneer,* June 2002.

9. Keenan, 5.

10. McGraw, 46.

11. St. Ignatius of Loyola, spiritual master from the sixteen century, encourages us to seek the grace to choose what is more for the glory of God, to choose whatever will better serve God. The desire to choose what is more for the glory of God will be the underlying motivation for accepting or relinquishing anything. Ignatius' principle of the "more," the Magis, means that one will be willing to do what is necessary, be willing to give up whatever stands in the way of giving greater glory to God (paraphrasing the Spiritual Exercises of St. Ignatius, #152). When applied to the vocation of marriage, our choices—what we do, what we accept or relinquish—will be determined by whatever is for the greater good of the marriage, and ultimately for the greater glory of God. (See also John English, *Spiritual Freedom: From an Experience of the Ignatian Exercises to the Art of Spiritual Direction* [Guelph, Ontario: Loyola House, 1973], 179.)

12. John Gray, *Men Are from Mars, Women Are from Venus: A Practical Guide for Improving Communication and Getting What You Want in Your Relationships* (New York: HarperCollins, 1992), 97–98, 112.

13. Gray, 69–76.

14. May Sarton, *Recovering: A Journal* (New York: Norton & Company, 1982), 115.

15. Gray, 206–244.

16. Shmuley Boteach, *Kosher Sex: A Recipe for Passion and Intimacy* (New York: Doubleday, 1999), 15–62.

17. Thomas Merton, quoted in *Weavings*, July/August 2002, 22.

CHAPTER 12

For Love or Money

Where your treasure is, there your heart will be also.
(Luke 12:34)

Money is the cause of many conflicts between married couples, and when the marriage combines two families, the conflicts are likely to be significantly more complex and emotionally intense. How married couples handle money can be an opportunity for growth or a major stumbling block to their happiness.

The way we approach money is in part influenced by our past. Insecurities and fears surrounding monetary issues are common. Financial decisions can be wrought with fear, anger, resentment, selfishness, and guilt. If we want to keep financial matters from controlling our marriage, we have to acknowledge and be prepared to deal with our emotions regarding money. We need to turn down the emotional dial and tend to financial considerations from the standpoint of reality.

According to clinical psychologist and syndicated columnist Val Farmer, the way couples handle money indicates the quality of their marriage.[1] Communication, with both spouses taking mutual responsibility, is of utmost importance. In addition to their day-to-day financial decisions, stepfamilies must deal with a variety of other issues: child support, alimony, any previous mortgages and loans, the possibility of a need for a larger home, and greater expenses. I shudder to think back to our family's grocery bills. Every week I loaded up the second refrigerator with twelve gallons of milk!

Financial issues have the power to dominate the mood of a family. If they are not dealt with in an open, loving, and fair manner, they can become a dark cloud that oppresses the family. Over time, unresolved issues involving money can erode the trust and intimacy between the most loving of couples.

Money and Our Relationships

Author Bernard Poduska, a professor of marriage, family, and human development at Brigham Young University, believes that there is a direct connection between the way family resources are allocated and the nature of the bond between a married couple: the allocation of their money reflects their values and priorities.[2] Are they primarily interested in meeting their own needs or in meeting the needs of others?

Poduska describes five different styles of resource allocation that can help us recognize when we are operating from a less-than-generous stance and can inspire us to a more loving approach. These are selfishness, convenience, commitment, charity, and devotion. Each style reflects a set of attitudes regarding commitment to one's spouse.

—The *selfishness* style of resource allocation is directed toward satisfying one's own needs without taking into account the needs of the spouse. A selfish relationship is based on "getting rather than giving." It could be summed up with this attitude: "I can do what I want. It's my money. I earned it."

—The *convenience* style occurs when one spouse is allowed only limited access to the other's resources. Only when it is convenient to do so will the other spouse's needs be met. There is no willingness to sacrifice if it is not convenient or if there is a fear of running short of funds. The message here is "You're not important!" The spouse quickly learns that he or she is not a top priority. In time, that spouse may seek other ways to feel important, even withdrawing from the relationship.

—In the *commitment* style, there is a willingness on the part of each spouse to give unlimited access to his or her resources, even when it may be inconvenient. Neither spouse's needs take precedence over the other's. Reciprocity and balance are the key elements of this style. The style of commitment requires an attitude of complete trust, since each spouse is vulnerable to the other. Each spouse must be willing to trust that he or she will not be exploited and that the family's resources will not be misused. In this style, Poduska explains, "the needs of others are considered to be at least as important as your own." The attitude that would summarize this style is "If I have it and you need it, then it's yours."

—In the *charity* style of allocation, when one spouse gives to the other, it is for the sheer pleasure of giving. No expectation of return clouds the happiness one experiences in giving to the other. There is no room for a ledger mentality in the charity style of allocation. Each willingly and joyfully gives to the other and even sacrifices for the other.

—The *devotion* style of allocation values the giving of one's time and attention even more than money. In this style, each partner actively seeks to meet the needs of the other, whatever those needs may be. Devotion is a true surrendering of oneself in loving the other, along with a willingness to be vulnerable and to expose oneself without any guarantee of being loved back. It is in this total giving of self that intimacy and authentic sacramental union grow.

Ultimately, if intimacy and authenticity are to grow, trust is the essential ingredient. If one spouse succumbs to the use of power, the marriage will not work. Only trust will yield the reward. As Poduska writes:

> If you trust the love in your relationship, you trust that the other person will not only try to satisfy your needs, but will also want you to have what would make you happy. Even when you have no way of obtaining what you seek, the person who loves you will still want you to have it. If, however, you do not trust the love in your relationship, you feel you must rely on yourself to satisfy your own needs. You rely more on power than on love. If the other person won't give you what you want, then you feel that you have to either get it yourself or manipulate the other person into getting it for you. In this case, you may succeed in getting what you want, but you can never succeed in making that other person want you to have it. Only when we love someone does his or her happiness become as important as our own.[3]

Examining Our Patterns of Consumption

How we deal with money indicates what we value in life. Does our emphasis on material acquisition reflect the priority of God and family in our lives, or does the way we live and spend money give the message to our children that the most important things in our lives are money, possessions, and power? Marcus Borg, in his book *Meeting Jesus Again for the First Time*, succinctly expresses our contemporary dilemma:

> Our culture's secular wisdom does not affirm the reality of the spirit. . . . It looks to the material world for satisfaction and meaning. Its dominant values are what I call the three A's—Achievement, Affluence, and Appearance. We live our lives in accord with these

values. We have the experience of being satiated, and yet we are still hungry.[4]

As parents, we need to look at our relationship with money. We need to examine what values our patterns of consumption impart to our children. Children in a stepfamily already must deal with the emotional pain of the changes in their family of origin. We must not set them up for an even greater sense of emptiness by handing them a legacy of idolatrous materialism.

A disconcerting realization of mine in the last few years is how insidiously I have been seduced into the over-consumption that characterizes our culture. I am disappointed with myself that my spending habits are not always in alignment with the values that I hold most precious. I feel a deep call to change this, to become more conscious of how and why I spend money.

Some Special Financial Considerations

Let's face it—stepfamilies are complicated! The couple's children may have come from one or both of the spouses' previous marriages and even from the couple's own marriage. Some of the children may have suffered the death of a biological parent, while others may have a noncustodial parent who is living and is more or less involved in their lives. An additional complication might be that some stepchildren whose biological parents have died, are ill, or are unfit would be adopted by a stepparent. Given this range of circumstances, it is understandable that the death of one of the spouses in a stepfamily has the potential for unleashing incredible emotional turmoil. So it is especially important to consider how children will be cared for and assets will be dispersed when a husband or wife dies—and this should be done, if possible, before the marriage takes place. This may sound unpleasant, but to deny the difficult reality or fail to deal with it could prove far more troublesome.

Prenuptial agreements are one option to consider. They can eliminate misunderstandings and will provide a stepparent with a safe, conflict-free transition with stepchildren after a spouse dies. Such agreements can guarantee a fair distribution, provide the surviving spouse with a fair entitlement of resources, and preserve assets from the previous marriage for the heirs of that marriage. The establishment of a trust may also achieve an equitable disbursement of resources. When considering assets, the couple should also take into consideration personal items such as jewelry, objects of art, family heirlooms, and other items such as silver, crystal, and china. It is helpful if the recipient of each specific item is clearly designated.

Do prenuptial agreements violate the spirit of a sacramental marriage? It depends on the spirit in which they are made. If each partner enters into the agreement willingly, and if it is undertaken out of love for the surviving spouse and children rather than so that one partner can control the other, then I believe it can be in the spirit of the sacrament.

Whether or not they enter into a prenuptial agreement, couples who are forming a stepfamily should immediately make a will. A great deal of heartache and resentment can be avoided by making each spouse's wishes clear about who should receive what in the event of his or her death. Even more important, without a will all of the deceased spouse's assets are likely to be awarded in trust to his or her children, leaving the surviving spouse with no resources to use to take care of the family. Care of the deceased's biological children who have a surviving biological parent must also be considered. In a stepfamily as well as in any family, preparations need to be made for care of the children in the event that both parents die. The issues are complex, and couples should seek the advice of a lawyer when considering how to handle these difficult questions.

Death is a fact of life, and making preparations for how our assets will be dispersed when we die is another way that we show our stepfamily that we love them. Money can't buy happiness, as the saying goes, but it can go along way toward paying bills and providing college educations. And by ensuring that our children will receive objects to which they have attached emotional significance, we will leave them with a reminder of our love while we also help them heal. By making our wishes clear, we can perhaps avoid the resentment that many families feel when they think that assets have been distributed unfairly. Our surviving spouse and children will have a difficult road ahead of them when we are gone. We should do everything we possibly can to smooth their journey.

To Work Outside the Home or Not?

The domestic labor and parenting provided by a stepmother in the home is immeasurably valuable to the well-being of the entire family. Her willingness to serve in this capacity can make the difference in whether the stepfamily is successful. Any family can stand only so much stress. When both spouses work outside the home, great demands are placed on the entire family.

The decision for the stepmother to work outside the home is important, and each couple's situation is unique. I was faced with a difficult choice. I was a nurse anesthetist earning a good salary. I enjoyed my work immensely. Anesthesia, however, is a very stressful profession, and I did not see how I could possibly care for a large family and continue my career while still maintaining my sanity! Our situation fortunately did not require me to work, but many families cannot get by without two incomes. The size of the family and the ages of the children will also enter into the decision. The point is that each spouse's contribution is of equal value in the family venture.

The Bottom Line

Finally, in financial jargon, "What's the bottom line?"

The bottom line is love, not money! Our relationships do not succeed if we are ledger oriented and power driven. Situations vary; styles of financial management vary; each couple and family have different needs.

Initially the financial aspect of my marriage was a painful area for me. My husband and I have very different personalities. I am intuitive and emotional, and he is practical and objective. I had to learn to trust and accept his style of decision making. There are many ways of loving. One of the major difficulties of a marriage that combines two families is that the couple has not had the luxury of an initial growth period before the children arrive. They do not have even the normal gestation period of nine months! They are immediately thrust into a nearly unmanageable situation, dealing with children traumatized by death or divorce. The newly married couple has to deal with enormous challenges. There is no time or space in which they can get to know each other and can come to understand the expression of love that is being offered. Their ways of loving each other can differ greatly, and their time of discovery is, to say the least, encumbered! My husband shows his love by taking care of things. He is thorough, has a strong sense of closure, and sincerely wants to do his best for all of us. He moves ahead, does things well, and gets things done! I had never been loved in this way.

From the time I was a teenager, I had to look out for myself, earn my own living, and do my own managing. So when Leonard took charge of our family's finances, I interpreted his actions as controlling, and I felt excluded. But I persisted in praying for trust, understanding, and growth. I realized that handling our financial affairs was an important need for him as well as a way of showing his love for me and our family. I now see his objective managerial style of dealing with our finances as rooted in devotion and coming from his heart. I feel secure in his love; he is my treasure.

Responsible, unselfish financial decisions may not be simple, but the call of God is clear. We must choose to love:

As God's chosen ones, holy and beloved, clothe yourselves with compassion, kindness, humility, meekness, and patience. Bear with one another and, if anyone has a complaint against another, forgive each other; just as the Lord has forgiven you, so you also must forgive. Above all, clothe yourselves with love, which binds everything together in perfect harmony. (Colossians 3:12-14)

For Your Personal Growth

Exercises:

1. Reflect on your expenditures for the past month or several months. How have your choices reflected your values?

2. Reflecting on the five styles of resource allocation, grade yourself on the degree to which each style reflects your attitudes, where 1 is "not at all" and 5 is "completely."

Selfishness	1	2	3	4	5
Convenience	1	2	3	4	5
Commitment	1	2	3	4	5
Charity	1	2	3	4	5
Devotion	1	2	3	4	5

What do your responses tell you?

3. Are there areas in which you need to change your attitude and perspective regarding money?

4. Are you encumbered with emotional issues that influence your financial decisions and/or discussions about money?

5. Are you comfortable with the allocation of resources within your family? If not, what are your options? How can you proceed?

Scripture:

Let these words of Jesus inspire and support your choice to foster mutuality and devotion in your marriage:

This is my commandment, that you love one another as I have loved you. No one has greater love than this, to lay down one's life for one's friends. (John 15:12-13)

NOTES

1. Val Farmer, "Attitude about Money Is a Test of Love," October 25, 1999, www.valfarmer.com.

2. Bernard E. Poduska, *For Love & Money: How to Share the Same Checkbook and Still Love Each Other* (Salt Lake City: Deseret Book Company, 1993), 78–81.

3. Poduska, 71–72.

4. Marcus J. Borg, *Meeting Jesus Again for the First Time: The Historical Jesus & the Heart of Contemporary Faith* (New York: HarperCollins, 1994), 87.

CHAPTER 13

The Gaze of Love

To lovingly gaze at a child is to pray for that child. To really look at our children and stepchildren—to look at them with sustained attention—is to open ourselves to the revelation of their preciousness.

All of us cry out to be truly seen. It is the cry of Emily Gibbs in Thornton Wilder's 1938 Pulitzer Prize–winning play, *Our Town*. Emily has died while giving birth to her second child. She meets her deceased mother-in-law, Mrs. Gibbs, and tells her that she wants to return to the land of the living for just one day. Despite Mrs. Gibbs' warning, Emily insists on returning so that she can watch herself living that day. She chooses her twelfth birthday. She is delighted to be in her childhood home, to see her mother preparing breakfast and her father reading the morning paper. She is astounded to find her parents so young and beautiful. Emily is overwhelmed with love and feels she cannot look at her world or her parents long and hard enough. They are so dear, and there is so little time.

As Emily watches her parents joyously surprising her with birthday gifts, she is overcome with a sense of urgency: "Oh, Mama, just look at me one minute as though you really saw me. . . . Mama, just for a moment we're happy. Let's look at one another." Emily breaks down, sobbing. "I can't. I can't go on. It goes so fast. We don't have time to look at one another. I didn't realize. So all that was going on and we never noticed. . . . Oh, earth, you're too wonderful for anybody to realize you. Do any human beings ever realize life while they live it?"[1]

Our children and stepchildren echo Emily's cry: "Just look at me one minute as though you really saw me." Emily entreats us to really look and see the miraculous wonder and beauty of our children and stepchildren. In the words of the poet Gerard Manley Hopkins, there is within their young hearts "the dearest freshness deep down"[2] that yearns to be revealed.

Praying for Our Stepchildren with Our Hearts

By looking with a sustained loving gaze, we discover the inner spirits of our stepchildren. Through our thoughtful, caring focus we become aware of the unique way God dwells within them. We instinctively lift them up to God, to the loving gaze of God who sees all, who knows what is best for them and who desires for them all goodness and life. This is a contemplative way of praying for them. Author May Sarton beautifully expresses the gift that gazing attentively bestows on us:

> If one looks long enough at almost anything, looks with absolute attention at a flower, a stone, the bark of a tree, grass, snow, a cloud, something like revelation takes place. Something is 'given,' and perhaps that something is always a reality outside the self. We are aware of God only when we cease to be aware of ourselves, not in the negative sense of denying the self, but in the sense of losing self in admiration and joy.[3]

When we allow ourselves to gaze unconditionally with absolute attention, we begin to see our stepchildren as they truly are, not as we may presume them to be. It is easy to see only what we want to see. We are quick to see the joy of their youth, the determination of their young minds, the resiliency of their able bodies.

However, it takes a sustained gaze to see beyond the obvious, to see more deeply into their young souls. We slowly become aware of the slight tentative gestures of insecurity they make. We see the hesitancy of their fear and the confusion of their grief, with all its attendant anger. We become aware of their gifts—a passion for reading, a love of music and art, an enjoyment of sports and play. We grow in appreciation of their innate desire to please us and be accepted. Only in looking deeply can we truly "see."

To pray for others, wordlessly and from the heart, is to be deeply present to them. Madeleine L'Engle, in her novel *A Wind in the Door*, describes how angels communicate. L'Engle tells us that angels relate to us heart to heart, spirit to spirit. Words are not necessary. She uses the word "kythe" to name this special way in which the angels make their presence felt within us.[4] As defined in *Jamieson's Scottish Dictionary*, "kythe" means "to be manifest, to appear without disguise."

This is a beautiful way for a mother or stepmother to pray for her children and/or stepchildren. I have discovered such a wordless prayer to be very helpful in my desire to understand, feel compassion for, and grow closer to my stepchildren. Here is how it works:

Choose the stepchild for whom you wish to pray.

Breathe slowly in and out a few times. Feel your body relax and your muscles lose their tension. Focus on relaxing each part of your body: your face, your shoulders, your chest and stomach, your arms and hands, your legs and feet. Put all other thoughts out of your mind. Only this prayer holds your attention.

Form the image of your stepchild in your imagination. Look attentively at him or her. What facial expression is present? Is it an expression of peace, confidence, and security, or is it an expression of fear, insecurity, or confusion? What posture do you see? Is it a posture of tentativeness, a posture of aggression, or a posture of anticipation? Look more deeply and see your stepchild as he or she truly is. Be present to your stepchild as you truly are. Desire for your stepchild the desire God has for him or her, the desire for all goodness and grace. Breathe the breath of compassion and unconditional love through your heart into the heart of your stepchild.

Continue in this manner, looking deeply at your stepchild in your mind and breathing through your heart to his or her heart the breath of love, the breath of God's love. See your stepchild surrounded with a gentle glow of light. The light is the healing light of God, and it is sending its rays of healing energy deep within your stepchild's spirit. This healing light of God's love will remain deep within your stepchild's spirit; it will guide and protect him or her.

Finally, picture the two of you together, bathed in God's light of unconditional love and acceptance. The light is warm, and its strength radiates through your bodies. It is an energy that bestows hope and encouragement. You turn toward each other and smile. You reach over and take your stepchild's hand in your own. You are embraced and united within God's healing energy of love.[5]

Actively Seeking God's Help

There are also moments when we may want to speak to God of our concern for our stepchildren, to ask in a more active way for God's help in a particular situation. It is not that we expect God to do things our way but that we request strength and help for ourselves or others to accept and trust that he will be present in the circumstance or event we are concerned about. I ask God that their hearts will be opened to the creative plan and energy with which the Holy Spirit has already graced them—because I know as a matter of faith that they already have what they need in order to live their lives fully. This is the attitude I find most freeing as I turn to God.

I have grown up with the belief that it is important to pray for those we love: our spouse, children, stepchildren, extended family, and friends. I believe it is also important to extend our intercessory prayer beyond our immediate circle and include the needs of our local, national, and global communities as well as to pray for this wondrous earth that we call our home. The list can get very long! Praying for others is an integral part of community, a way of supporting and bonding with each other. To pray for others is a uniting of intention.

Many traditions recognize the wise and holy people who have gone before them, the community of saints who have died and are enjoying a greater intimacy with God. Individuals may prayerfully request a saint's help in asking God to hear their prayers and meet their needs. The premise is that these holy people have a wonderful access to God, so God will surely hear their prayers! None of us fully understands life after death, but we believe that the spirits of our loved ones continue to live and are, in some mysterious way, closer to God, gazing on God, than those of us who are still living our earthly lives.

My paternal grandmother was a gentle and holy woman who strove all her life to serve and to praise God. I am certain that her spirit is being held within the loving and compassionate embrace of God, where she abides in deep friendship and peace. I never hesitate to call on her to intercede on my behalf. God would never deny her, I am sure! I believe that God hears all our prayers, but it doesn't hurt to gather a little more steam, to storm the heavens with all the powerful prayers we can garner.

I have called upon the saints to intercede for me since I was a little girl. A life of prayer frequently grows out of desperate need, and as a young girl there were times when I felt very desperate. When my father would come home intoxicated and violent, I would run upstairs and pray to St. Jude to help my family, to save us from Daddy's anger, and to help him quit drinking. On the day I was confirmed, I received as my patron saint Therese of Lisieux, known as the Little Flower. She became St. Jude's companion in interceding for me with the Lord. Now, many years later, I am still asking St. Jude and St. Therese to join with me in petitioning God to help me and those I love.

I have found as I have aged, however, that my prayers have become more contemplative. I seem to make fewer specific requests of God now, perhaps because experience and hindsight have shown me that my proposed solutions weren't always the best. I have learned to entrust my cares to God and ask that he give all of us the strength we need to deal with the challenges life presents. For time and again God, in his wisdom, has shown me that his response to my loved ones' needs—and his timetable for bringing it about—are greatly superior to my own.

It seems as if God continues to teach me with that lesson. Twenty-three years ago, I became very distressed when, because of a series of extenuating circumstances, my youngest son was not confirmed at the customary age of thirteen. I have a firm belief in the special graces that the Holy Spirit confers through the Sacrament of Confirmation and had prayed daily that my son would be confirmed—and the sooner the better! Years went by, and it seemed as if God wasn't hearing my prayer. God's timetable may have been very different than mine, but he did answer my prayer. At the age of thirty-four, my son was confirmed with his wife, who is joining him in his Catholic faith. During the first ritual of the preparation, the candidates were asked why they wanted to receive the Sacrament of Confirmation. My son jokingly told me that he replied, "My mother told me to!"

Years ago I came upon the following prayer by an unknown author. It has sustained me through many worrisome and frightening times, reminding me that God has already graced my loved ones with everything they need to live holy lives.

Prayer of Letting Go

To a dear one about whom I have been concerned,
I behold the Christ in you.
I place you lovingly in the care of the Father.
I release you from my anxiety and concern.
I let go of my possessive hold on you.
I am willing to free you to live your life
according to your best light and understanding.
My child (stepchild, husband, wife, friend, etc.)
I no longer try to force my ideas on you,
my ways on you.
I lift my thoughts above you, above the personal level.
I see you as God sees you, a spiritual being, created
in his image, and endowed with qualities and abilities
that make you needed, and important
not only to me but to God and God's larger plan
I do not bind you, I no longer believe that you do not have
the understanding you need in order to meet life.
I bless you.
I have faith in you.
I behold Jesus in you.

God Will Not Abandon Us or Our Children

Over the years I have grown to trust that God knows the needs of those I love. After all, our Father loves them even more than I do. He has never abandoned me, and he will not abandon them.

Within all the circumstances and events of my life, through all the valleys and hills, fire and flames, God has accompanied me. The lessons I have been destined to learn have not always been easy or pleasant, but our Lord's presence has broken through every struggle, miraculously manifesting itself according to the needs of the situation. Christ's presence often comes in the form of just the right word of kindness, counsel, or direction, or even the right person at the right time. On occasion it has come as an incredibly fortunate series of events or as a flashing light of insight. God's presence has touched me beautifully through the sound of music, the wonders of nature, the miracle of love, and even the gentle devotion of my golden retriever. All these manifestations of God's love have graced me with solace, comfort, healing, guidance, wisdom, and most of all gratitude and trust.

Our God is an everlastingly faithful, loving God. Even if we should somehow fail those who have been entrusted to our love and care, God will not abandon them. The prophet Isaiah beautifully expresses this enduring promise:

> *Can a woman forget her nursing child,*
> *or show no compassion for the child of her womb?*
> *Even these may forget,*
> *yet I will not forget you.* (Isaiah 49:15)

Growth in trust always moves one toward deeper interior silence; it is a natural progression. I remember that when Leonard and I were just beginning to develop a relationship, we were always talking. That nearly constant exchange of ideas, feelings, and opinions was necessary in order to get to know each other. But after some time, when our relationship had grown, our trust in each other had also grown. Now we can sit lovingly silent with each other, content and confident in each other's presence.

I find that this movement toward silence is also true in my relationship with God. As trust grows, my prayer grows quieter; my praying for others grows less specific. I do not mean to imply that quieter is necessarily better; there are different seasons in life, different moments, and different patterns of prayer emerge from those seasons and moments. For now I am content and confident to gaze at those I love and to lift them to God's gaze.

To lovingly gaze at your stepchild is to pray for your stepchild.

Listen to the cry, "Look at me as though you really see me."

For Your Personal Growth

Exercises:

1. Gently gaze at your stepchild sometime soon. Look at him or her with your absolute attention. What is the gift of your gaze?

2. Think of someone about whom you are concerned. Daily pray the "Letting Go" prayer for him or her.

3. Use the gazing prayer of love for each member of your family.

Scripture:

We have evidence in Scripture that Jesus looked with love, gazed intently, on those for whom he had a special care. When a rich man asked what he must do to inherit eternal life,

Jesus, **looking at him, loved him** *and said, "You lack one thing; go, sell what you own, and give the money to the poor, and you will have treasure in heaven; then come, follow me."* (Mark 10:21)

After Peter had denied Jesus three times, as Jesus had predicted,

[t]he Lord turned and **looked at Peter.** *. . . And [Peter] went out and wept bitterly.* (Luke 22:61-62)

Consider what it would have been like to have been looked at intently by Jesus.

NOTES

1. Thornton Wilder, *Our Town* (New York: Harper & Row, 1957), Act III, 101–129, Special contents copyright, Franklin Mint Corporation, 1980.

2. Gerard Manley Hopkins, "God's Grandeur," *Poems and Prose* (London: Penguin Books, 1953), 27.

3. May Sarton, *Journal of a Solitude: The Intimate Diary of a Year in the Life of a Creative Woman* (New York: Norton & Company, 1973), 99.

4. Madeleine L'Engle, *A Wind in the Door* (New York: Dell Publishing, 1973), 88.

5. Louis M. Savary and Patricia H. Berne, *Kything: The Art of Spiritual Presence* (New York: Paulist Press, 1988).

The Myth of the Phoenix Bird

*Christ was raised from the dead . . . that we too might live
a new life. (Romans 6:4, paraphrased)*

The myth of the phoenix bird is an ancient resurrection story
that speaks powerfully of death and new beginnings. For Christians, the bird symbolizes the dying and rising of Christ. Its message of hope calls us, as stepmothers, to trust in the transforming
power of love. The myth opens the way for seeing the breakdowns
and breakthroughs that are integral to building a family. Through
its lens, we can see our role as stepmothers in a new light—one of
creating security where there was anxiety, hope where there was
despair, family where there was fragmentation. Here is how the
story goes:

Once upon a time in a faraway place in the East, there lived a
bird of unimaginable beauty. I first saw her flying in the golden
orb of the sun, her head poised and majestic. She was incredibly
magnificent. Her colorful wings shimmered so brightly that they
nearly surpassed the sun's radiance. The red and purple of her tail
feathers swept out behind her like a bridal train. I watched in utter
amazement. I felt my heart open to receive and savor the spectacular beauty of this unusual bird.

As I watched, she came to rest in my garden and fed on the
morning dew. During the night I listened for her, and in the morning I hurried to catch a glimpse of her to see if she had returned.

Day gave way to day and night to night. And yet, I never tired at the sight of her; my heart was filled with love. In the timelessness of my love, time itself seemed fulfilled. The bird became ever more brilliant, more beautiful, and more radiant.

Then one morning the great bird alighted at the topmost branches of the tallest tree in my garden. I do not know when she did it or how, but there among the full branches was a large and fragrant nest of precious herbs and spices. I watched intently as the great bird circled the entire garden and came to rest peacefully in the nest.

I watched the golden bird throughout the entire day. My eyes remained fixed on her. Through the rosy hue of the morning sun, I watched. In the unrelenting brilliance of the noonday sun, I watched. Through the early shadows of the late afternoon, I watched. My eyes were constant in their vigilance. As evening slowly descended, the magnificent bird rested in stillness, her golden feathers catching the rays of the setting sun.

Then, just as the sun disappeared below the western horizon, the nest burst into flames. The great and beautiful bird did not move. She allowed herself to be engulfed in flames that leapt up and surrounded her without mercy. For a brief moment, forever impressed on my memory, the life of the fire and the life of the bird were one, indistinguishable. The bird was being consumed within the fire's power. The night air was permeated by the spicy scent of the burned nest. I breathed in its sweet incense. My eyes continued to gaze upward at what was now merely a glowing coal. The magnificent bird was gone.

My heart was filled with grief. In my sorrow, sleep escaped me. Why did such a beautiful bird have to die? The question resonated within my heart throughout the long night. Morning found me weeping. I was in despair.

Something deep within me impelled me to look at the charred nest. Slowly I became aware of a gentle glow radiating from the remains of the great bird and her nest. As I watched, the glow became brighter and brighter.

Then suddenly within the center of the light, there appeared a small bird, which as I watched took on the same brilliance and color of the great bird I had grown to know and love.

For three long and wonder-filled days, I watched the new bird. Without taking food or water, I watched. I saw the bird grow stronger. I saw her trying out her new wings, testing her strength. I gloried in the already regal poise of the bird, her noble head, and her eyes that held a concentrated and intense purpose.

On the morning of the third day, just as the sun was rising, the still small yet magnificent bird rallied all her strength. Lifting herself above the nest containing the remains of her mother, she flew unfalteringly toward the horizon and disappeared into the rising sun.

I am alone now. Was it only a dream? No, it was not a dream. The fragrant presence of the magnificent bird remains within me. My heart reassures me that the strength and beauty of its dying and the wonder of the new birth will remain always a part of me.

In spirit, my being kneels before such a great and powerful event.[1]

For Your Personal Growth

Questions for reflection:

1. How does the myth symbolize the new life that issued forth after the divorce or death that led to your remarriage and the creation of your new family?

2. How does the myth symbolize the ongoing daily ups and downs of your stepfamily as it struggles and grows?

Scripture:

As you read the promise offered by Christ in John 12:24, let your heart be filled with hope and peace. Be confident that every sincere effort, every sacrifice made in love, will abundantly bear fruit:

Very truly, I tell you, unless a grain of wheat falls into the earth and dies, it remains just a single grain; but if it dies, it bears much fruit.

NOTES

1. Francis X. Glimm, Joseph M. F. Marique, and Gerald G. Walsh, trans., *The Apostolic Fathers*, vol. 1 of *The Fathers of the Church* (New York: CIMA Publishing Co., 1947), 30.

Resources for Stepfamilies

Beginning Experience International Ministry (grief resolution for adults and children who have suffered loss through death or divorce)
1657 Commerce Drive
South Bend, IN 46628
Phone: 866-610-8877 (toll free in US and Canada)
E-mail: beginningexperience@earthlink.net
www.beginningexperience.org

Contemplative Outreach (centering prayer)
P.O. Box 737
10 Park Place, Suite 2B
Butler, NJ 07405
Phone: 973-838-3384
E-mail: office@coutreach.org
www.contemplativeoutreach.org

Worldwide Marriage Encounter (for marriage enrichment)
2210 East Highland Avenue, Suite 106
San Bernardino, CA 92404-4666
Phone: 909-863-9963
E-mail: office@wwme.org
www.wwme.org/index.html

Retrouvaille (for troubled marriages)
Phone: 800-470-2230
www.retrouvaille.org

Retreats International
P.O. Box 1067
Notre Dame, IN 46556
Phone: 574-247-4443
E-mail: retreatsintl@sbcglobal.net
www.retreatsintl.org

Spiritual Directors International
P.O. Box 3584
Bellevue, WA 98009-3584
Phone: 425-455-1565
E-mail: office@sdiworld.org
www.sdiworld.org

Stepfamily Association of America
650 J Street, Suite 205
Lincoln, NE 68508
Phone: 800-735-0329
E-mail: stepfams@aol.com
www.saafamilies.org

STEP-Carefully! (Christian ministry dedicated to applying Christ's teachings for family dynamics to stepfamilies)
P.O. Box 10918
Fort Smith, AR 72917-0918
Phone: 479-522-7490
E-mail: step@stepcarefully.com
www.stepcarefully.com

Bibliography

Balke, Most Reverend Victor H. *Be Compassionate*. Pastoral Letter, July 3, 1980. available from the Diocese of Crookston, 1200 Memorial Drive, Crookston, MN 56716. E-mail: askus@crookston.org.

Bartocci, Barbara. *Nobody's Child Anymore: Grieving, Caring, and Comforting When Parents Die*. Notre Dame, In.: Sorin Books, 2000.

Becker, Marty, with Danelle Morton. *The Healing Power of Pets: Harnessing the Amazing Ability of Pets to Make and Keep People Happy and Healthy*. New York: Hyperion, 2002.

Bergan, Jacqueline Syrup, and Marie Schwan. *Love; Forgiveness; Birth*. Ijamsville, Md.: The Word Among Us Press, 2003–2004.

Bergan, Jacqueline Syrup, and Marie Schwan. *Praying with Ignatius of Loyola*. Ijamsville, Md.: The Word Among Us Press, 2003.

Bergan, Jacqueline Syrup, and Marie Schwan. *Take and Receive*. 5 vols. Winona, Minn.: St. Mary's Press, 1985–1988.

Bernhard, Emery. *The Girl Who Wanted to Hunt: A Siberian Tale*. New York: Holiday House, 1994.

Bettelheim, Bruno. *The Uses of Enchantment: The Meaning and Importance of Fairy Tales*. New York: Alfred A. Knopf, 1976.

Borg, Marcus J. *Meeting Jesus Again for the First Time: The Historical Jesus & the Heart of Contemporary Faith*. New York: HarperCollins, 1994.

Boteach, Shmuley. *Kosher Sex: A Recipe for Passion and Intimacy*. New York: Doubleday, 1999.

Bray, James, and John Kelly. *Stepfamilies: Love, Marriage, and Parenting in the First Decade*. New York: Broadway Books, 1998.

Clark, J. M. *Meister Eckhart: An Introduction to the Study of His Works with an Anthology of His Sermons*. London: Thomas Nelson & Sons, 1957.

Clinton, Hillary Rodham. *It Takes a Village and Other Lessons Children Teach Us*. New York: Simon & Schuster, 1996.

Covey, Stephen R. *The 7 Habits of Highly Effective Families*. New York: Golden Books, 1997.

Cowan, Marian, and John Carroll Futrell. *The Spiritual Exercises of St. Ignatius of Loyola: A Handbook for Directors*. New York: Le Jacq Publishing, 1982.

Cummings, E. E. *Collected Poems*. Franklin Center, Pa.: The Franklin Library, 1977.

Daly, Martin, and Margo Wilson. *The Truth about Cinderella, A Darwinian View of Parental Love*. New Haven: Yale University Press, 1998.

Day, Nancy Raines. *The Lion's Whiskers: An Ethiopian Folktale*. New York: Scholastic, 1995.

"Divorce Statistics Collection." www.divorcereform.org/stats.html.

Dupleix, André. *15 Days of Prayer with Pierre de Chardin*. Liguori, Mo.: Liguori Publications, 1999.

Edelman, Hope. *Motherless Daughters: The Legacy of Loss*. New York: Dell Publishing, 1994.

English, John. *Spiritual Freedom: From an Experience of the Ignatian Exercises to the Art of Spiritual Direction*. Guelph, Ontario: Loyola House, 1973.

Faber, Adele, and Elaine Mazlish. *How to Talk So Kids Will Listen and Listen So Kids Will Talk*. New York: HarperCollins, 1999.

Farmer, Val. "Attitude about Money Is a Test of Love." October 25, 1999. www.valfarmer.com.

Farmer, Val. "Stepfathers Must Get Off to the Right Start." *Pioneer,* June 2002.

Finley, James. *Christian Meditation: Experiencing the Presence of God*. New York: HarperCollins, 2004.

Finley, James. *The Contemplative Heart*. Notre Dame, In.: Sorin Books, 2000.

Fleming, David L. *A Contemporary Reading of the Spiritual Exercises: A Companion to St. Ignatius' Text.* St. Louis: Institute of Jesuit Sources, 1976.

Foster, Michael Smith. *Annulment: the Wedding That Was.* New York: Paulist Press, 1999.

Fox, Matthew. *Breakthrough: Meister Eckhart's Creation Spirituality in New Translation.* Garden City, N.Y.: Image Books, 1980.

Glimm, Francis X., Joseph M. F. Marique, and Gerald G. Walsh, trans. *The Apostolic Fathers.* Vol. 1 of *The Fathers of the Church.* New York: CIMA Publishing Co., 1947.

Gray, John. *Men Are from Mars, Women Are from Venus: A Practical Guide for Improving Communications and Getting What You Want in Your Relationships.* New York: HarperCollins, 1992.

Hanh, Thich Nhat. *The Blooming of a Lotus: Guided Meditation Exercises for Healing and Transformation.* Boston: Beacon Press, 1993.

Hanh, Thich Nhat. *The Present Moment: A Retreat on the Practice of Mindfulness.* audiocassettes. Boulder, Co.: Sounds True, 1994.

Harris, Maxine. *The Loss That Is Forever: The Lifelong Impact of the Early Death of a Mother or Father.* New York: Penguin Books, 1995.

Heskin, Kathy. *Marriage: A Spiritual Journey.* Mystic, Ct.: Twenty-Third Publications, 2002.

Hetherington, E. Mavis, and John Kelly. *For Better or for Worse: Divorce Reconsidered.* New York: Norton & Company, 2002.

Hopkins, Gerard Manley. *Poems and Prose.* London: Penguin Books, 1953.

Jager, Willigis. *The Way to Contemplation: Encountering God Today.* New York: Paulist Press, 1982.

Johnson, Robert A. *Inner Work: Using Dreams & Creative Imagination for Personal Growth and Integration.* San Francisco: Harper & Row, 1986.

Jung, C. G. trans., R. F. C. Hull. *Four Archetypes: Mother, Rebirth, Spirit, Trickster*. Princeton: Princeton University Press, 1967.

Kabat-Zinn, Jon. *Full Catastrophe Living: Using the Wisdom of Your Body and Mind to Face Stress, Pain, and Illness*. New York: Dell Publishing, 1990.

Keating, Thomas. *Open Mind, Open Heart: The Contemplative Dimension of the Gospel*. Amity, N.Y.: Amity House, 1986.

Keenan, Barbara Mullen. *When You Marry a Man with Children: How to Put Your Marriage First and Stay in Love*. New York: Simon & Schuster, 1992.

Kowalski, Gary. *The Souls of Animals*. Walpole, N.H.: Stillpoint Publishing, 1991.

Kubler-Ross, Elisabeth. *On Death and Dying*. New York: Macmillan, 1969.

Kung, Hans. trans., Edward Quinn. *On Being a Christian*. Garden City, N.Y.: Doubleday, 1976.

L'Engle, Madeleine. *A Wind in the Door*. New York: Dell Publishing, 1973.

Levang, Elizabeth. *When Men Grieve: Why Men Grieve Differently & How You Can Help*. Minneapolis: Fairview Press, 1998.

Linn, Dennis, and Matthew Linn. *Healing Life's Hurts: Healing Memories through the Five Stages of Forgiveness*. New York: Paulist Press, 1978.

Linn, Matthew, and Dennis Linn. *Healing of Memories*. New York: Paulist Press, 1974.

Maples, Fred. "Prayer of Petition," *Loyola Letter: A Spiritual Renewal Resource*. Spring 2000.

Marcus, Clare Cooper. *House as a Mirror of Self: Exploring the Deeper Meaning of Home*. Berkeley: Conari Press, 1997.

May, Rollo. *The Art of Counseling*. Nashville: Abingdon, 1967.

Mayers, Gregory. *Listen to the Desert: Secrets of Spiritual Maturity from the Desert Fathers and Mothers*. Liguori, Mo.: Liguori/Triumph, 1996.

McGraw, Phillip C. *Relationship Rescue: A Seven Step Strategy for Reconnecting with Your Partner.* New York: Hyperion, 2000.

Myss, Caroline. *Anatomy of the Spirit: The Seven Stages of Power and Healing.* New York: Harmony Books, 1992.

Myss, Caroline. *Sacred Contracts: Awakening Your Divine Potential.* audiocassette. Boulder: Sounds True Publishing Company, 2001.

Norris, Gunilla. *Being Home: Discovering the Spiritual in the Everyday.* Mahwah, N.J.: Hidden Spring, 2001.

Pennington, Basil M. *Centering Prayer: Renewing an Ancient Christian Prayer Form.* Garden City, N.Y.: Image Books, 1982.

Poduska, Bernard E. *For Love & Money: How to Share the Same Checkbook and Still Love Each Other.* Salt Lake City: Deseret Book Company, 1993.

Poduska, Bernard E. *Till Debt Do Us Part: Balancing Finances, Feeling, and Family.* Salt Lake City: Shadow Mountain, 2000.

Regniers, Beatrice Schenk de. *Little Sister and the Month Brothers.* New York: Lothrop, Lee & Shephard Books, 1967.

Rupp, Joyce. *Praying Our Goodbyes.* Notre Dame, In.: Ava Maria Press, 1988.

Russack. Neil. *Animal Guides in Life, Myth and Dreams.* Toronto: Inner City Books, 2002.

Sarton, May. *Journal of a Solitude: The Intimate Diary of a Year in the Life of a Creative Woman*: New York: Norton & Company, 1973.

Sarton, May. *Recovering: A Journal.* New York: Norton & Company, 1982.

Savary, Louis M., and Patricia H. Berne. *Kything: The Art of Spiritual Presence.* New York: Paulist Press, 1988.

Staudacher, Carol. *A Time to Grieve: Meditations for Healing After the Death of a Loved One.* New York: HarperCollins, 1994.

Stepfamily Association of America. "Stepfamily Facts." www.saafamilies.org/faqs/.

Tatar, Maria. *The Hard Facts of the Grimms' Fairy Tales*. Princeton: Princeton University Press, 1987.

Tolle, Eckhart. *The Power of Now: A Guide to Spiritual Enlightenment*. Novoto, Ca.: New World Library, 1999.

Tresidder, Jack. *Symbols and Their Meanings*. New York: Friedman/ Fairfax Publishers, 2000.

Van Kaam, Adrian. *Spirituality and the Gentle Life*. Denville, N.J.: Dimension Books, 1974.

Venable, Leslie Allgood. *The Not So Wicked Stepmother: A Book for Children and Adults*. Birmingham: L. A. Venable Publishing, 1998.

Von Franz, Marie-Louise. *Individuation in Fairy Tales*. Boston: Shambhala, 1990.

Von Franz, Marie-Louise. *Interpretation of Fairy Tales*. Dallas: Spring Publications, 1982.

Vries, Ad de. *Dictionary of Symbols and Imagery*. Amsterdam: North-Holland Publishing Company, 1984.

Wallerstein, Judith S., Julia Lewis, and Sandra Blakeslee. *The Unexpected Legacy of Divorce: A 25 Year Landmark Study*. New York: Hyperion, 2000.

Weavings. July/August 2002.

Wilder, Thornton. *Our Town*. New York: Harper & Row, 1957. Special contents copyright, Franklin Mint Corporation, 1980.

Woodman, Marion. *Addiction to Perfection: The Still Unravished Bride*. Toronto: Inner City Books, 1982.

Woodman, Marion. *The Pregnant Virgin: A Process of Psychological Transformation*. Toronto: Inner City Books, 1985.

Worden, J. William. *Children and Grief: When a Parent Dies*. New York: Guilford Press, 1996.

About the Author

Jacqueline Syrup Bergan, a stepmother for thirty-two years, is the coauthor of the highly acclaimed five-volume Take and Receive series (*Love, Forgiveness, Birth, Freedom,* and *Surrender*), which guides readers through the Spiritual Exercises of St. Ignatius. She has also coauthored *Praying with Ignatius of Loyola* and *Taste and See: Prayer Services for Gatherings of Faith*. Jacqueline has an extensive background leading retreats, parish days of renewal, and spirituality workshops and has offered private spiritual direction for many years. She and her husband Leonard have raised a blended family of eight children and have seventeen grandchildren. They live on Bear Trap Lake in Wisconsin and spend their winters in Rio Verde, Arizona.

Growing as a Stepmom—with God's Help!
Jacqueline Syrup Bergan

Here is a powerful testimony to the rewards and challenges of accepting God's call to love and nurture another woman's children. Jacqueline Bergan offers an honest, encouraging, and faith-filled glimpse into her thirty-two-year experience as mother and stepmother to a family of eight children. The Scripture passages, questions for reflection, and exercises included at the end of each chapter will help every stepmother to respond in love and prayer to the complexities of a blended family.

"Humor, love, and prayer combined with common sense, practical strategies, and a clear, understandable explanation of the stepmothering process all add up to a 'must read' for Christians on this journey."

Gabrielle Lawrence, Ph.D., licensed psychologist and Christian therapist, Scottsdale, Arizona

"This book is a treasure for any stepmother seeking God's wisdom and grace in her new role. The format is excellent for individual reflection or group sharing. A perfect gift for a new stepmother!"

Sr. Paula Hagen, OSB, National Director, Ministry of Mothers Sharing

"Jacqueline Bergan addressed all the areas of growth that I faced as a stepmom through the labor pains of creating a blessed stepfamily under the protection of God's wings."

Gail A. Hartman, mother and stepmother, Chandler, Arizona

Jacqueline Syrup Bergan is the coauthor of the highly acclaimed five-volume *Take and Receive Series* (*Love*, *Forgiveness*, *Birth*, *Freedom*, and *Surrender*), which guides readers through the Spiritual Exercises of St. Ignatius. She has an extensive background leading retreats and spirituality workshops and has offered private spiritual direction for many years.

ISBN 1-59325-053-3

the WORD among us®
www.wordamongus.org

9 781593 250539